T0171527

LISTEN UP, MR. PRESIDENT

Everything You Always Wanted Your President to Know and Do

Helen Thomas and *Craig Crawford*

SCRIBNER

New York   London   Toronto   Sydney

Scribner
A Division of Simon & Schuster, Inc.
1230 Avenue of the Americas
New York, NY 10020

First Scribner trade paperback edition October 2010

SCRIBNER and design are registered trademarks of The Gale Group, Inc., used
under license by Simon & Schuster, Inc., the publisher of this work.

For information about special discounts for bulk purchases, please contact Simon
& Schuster Special Sales at 1-866-506-1949 or business@simonandschuster.com.

The Simon & Schuster Speakers Bureau can bring authors to your live event. For
more information or to book an event, contact the Simon & Schuster Speakers
Bureau at 1-866-248-3049 or visit our website at www.simonspeakers.com.

Designed by Carla Jayne Jones

Manufactured in the United States of America

1   3   5   7   9   10   8   6   4   2

Library of Congress Control Number: 2009021609

ISBN 978-1-4391-4815-0
ISBN 978-1-4391-4816-7 (pbk)
ISBN 978-1-4391-5325-3 (ebook)

To the men and women who faithfully serve the public at all levels, from City Hall to the White House

CONTENTS

PREFACE

We love the American presidency and we want whoever is duly elected to the office to succeed. We wrote this book to help.

Presidents are fascinating people. We have covered quite a few as Washington journalists and we love it. For us, it hardly seems like a job. It's more like we're spectators at the greatest sporting event of all time: presidential politics.

For voters, politics is even better than sports—because they get to play.

The presidency is like the Emerson, Lake, and Palmer song says—the "show that never ends." No matter who is in office, the nature of the job makes the work and the people doing it endlessly interesting.

The idea for a presidential "lesson plan" came to us over the years as we regularly met for dinner with other friends to swap stories, compare notes, and share our opinions about what presidents do right and what they do wrong. And we found that we nearly always agreed on the basics of what makes a successful president.

So, we decided, why not share what we think with all future presidents, and in the process help voters understand a little more about what to look for when picking someone for the most powerful and challenging job in the world.

We are not presidential scholars, although we admire them and quote a few in these pages. We are journalists, and it has been said that journalists write the "first draft" of history.

Helen has directly covered more presidents than any journalist working today, starting as a White House correspondent in 1960 covering John F. Kennedy's new administration. But her reporting career began in 1945, at the end of Franklin Roosevelt's administration. She has written five books about the presidency and in August of 2008 was the subject of an HBO documentary about her White House coverage, titled *Thank You, Mr. President*.

Craig came to Washington as a journalist in the final days of Ronald Reagan's presidency and has covered every presidential campaign since 1988. As a college student he worked in the press office of Jimmy Carter's White House. Before becoming a journalist, he worked on the campaign staffs of presidential candidates. He has written two books on politics.

This book relies upon our own "first drafts" of history, garnered from our personal observations of the presidents we have covered, but it also relies upon the rich history of all presidents since George Washington. In every case, whether a modern or historical example, we looked for the lessons to be learned. Just imagine if past presidents came back to life and sat down for a chat with a new occupant of the Oval Office and said, Here's how to avoid our mistakes, or repeat our successes. We have tried here to be the "mediums," to channel their voices, to pass on their wisdom.

Rather than attempting to be a history text, this book is more about practical tips. Our advice is not limited to the current president, Barack Obama. Instead, we strove to find timeless lessons—and warnings—for anyone burdened with this office.

Why do we feel this sort of presidential advice is necessary? Because we have observed so many great and talented men enter the White House, full of ambitious enthusiasm from a winning campaign, only to be hit with the sobering realization that they might not know as much about the job as they thought they did.

Some found their way. Others did not. We thought it worth making the effort to come up with our own manual of sorts for easing that initial shock.

Most presidents do try to learn from their predecessors. Remembering those who came before you—and staying in contact with those who are still alive—helps remind the new president that, while it might be the loneliest job in the world, he is not the only one who has faced the pain and stress of being leader of the free world.

The best presidents are visionaries. John F. Kennedy laid the groundwork for sending astronauts to the moon, producing a national focus on science and technology that prepared the country to dominate the computer age.

Changing the country for the better is what good presidents do. Most monarchies in history ultimately collapsed because they were institutionally built to value and protect the status quo. Why wouldn't they? If you were king or queen for life and could pass it on to your heirs, would you want to be an agent of change?

The genius of our system is that we force the question of change every four years. No person or political party owns the presidency. Voters can keep things as they are if they're happy; if they're not, they can go with something entirely new.

Ultimately, the fate of American presidents is up to the voter. Thinking about the basic principles of success in the White House can help voters better understand the trials and tribulations that accompany the presidency.

Regardless of what happens with the Obama presidency—and it's way too soon to tell—his election in 2008 was a clear demonstration of how our still young county can refresh itself. The historic outpouring of new voters and young people getting their first experience as citizen activists showed the world that democracy works.

Obama's campaign mantra of "change" resonated with the millions of Americans disenchanted with the direction of the last administration. The election galvanized a deluge of voters who cast ballots for the first time and became involved in the campaigns and election process. After all, the future belongs to them.

The enthusiastic atmosphere on Election Day 2008 was so infectious it almost became a sin not to vote. When the results came in and Obama had won, a spontaneous crowd flocked to the White House despite a cold rain. Motorists honked their horns. Into the early hours of the next morning pedestrians in the nation's capital could be heard cheering.

We change presidents without guns and violent coups, and that is a hallmark of our democracy. If you boil it down, these young and new voters saw a new day with a new president with the leadership and courage to change our country. That is the great promise of the American presidency, and that is why we have tried in this book to develop a set of guidelines to help all new presidents and their supporters match the promise with deeds that get the job done.

One of the most awkward, and yet vital, moments in the White House is the day the newly elected president comes calling on the outgoing chief executive for the traditional tour of the mansion. These meetings always intrigue and inspire us as journalists. They are reminders of the continuity of the office, the passing of a torch that will hopefully burn bright and long.

These rather formal and stiff moments between the old and the new are especially tense when the new president has actually beaten the incumbent.

It was such a day in 1992 when newly elected Bill Clinton stepped into the Oval Office with President George H. W. Bush. As the reporters and photographers who had been ushered in to record the moment were preparing to leave, Bush invited Clinton to tour the president's house, and Clinton said, "You don't have to do this, Mr. President."

To which we replied, "Yes you do."

ACKNOWLEDGMENTS

The authors would like to acknowledge Scribner editor Samantha Martin for her keen wit and wisdom in shaping the concept and outcome of this book, David Blank for his critical research and editing skills, and, as always, our close friend and adviser Diane Nine for keeping us on the job.

ONE

BRACE YOURSELF:
THE WORST IS YET TO COME

As the term of my relief from this place [Washington, D.C.]
approaches, its drudgery becomes more nauseating
and intolerable.
—THOMAS JEFFERSON

Mr. President, your inauguration is likely to be the happiest day of your presidency. If only you could make that feeling last forever. The White House can be one of the loneliest places in the world. Just look at the physical deterioration some have suffered during their years in office.

Think about how bad it could get and know this: It will probably be worse. The glow of your inauguration will fade. It may take a week, or it may take a month; if you're lucky, it may take a bit longer, but it will happen.

The American presidency is sometimes called the most powerful job in the world. It might be more accurate to say it is the most stressful. Though you try to imagine what crisis or unexpected political event might turn your job into a nightmare, you won't be able to; you can only prepare for the worst and develop ways to cope.

Wars, economic calamity, natural disasters, and domestic unrest top the list of challenges that have made some presidents seem to age before our eyes over the span of a four-year term. (If you do not want more gray hair, be prepared for a dye job.) And some presidents never politically recover. Jimmy Carter lost reelection over a hostage crisis. Lyndon Johnson's presidency became a casualty of the Vietnam War. Richard Nixon resigned because of the Watergate scandal.

Ways to cope with a crisis range from seeking the counsel of your predecessors to keeping your sense of humor and making time for stress-relieving diversions (preferably not something politically disastrous, like adultery). Still, unreasonably high expectations inevitably lead to disappointment—for presidents and their public. Americans can never resist indulging the hope that a popular new president will change everything and make our problems go away. We might know in our guts that we're expecting too much, but our hearts want us to believe.

The job might be easier on presidents—and the rest of us, for that matter—if we were more realistic about how much a new president can really get done, and if we remember that something unexpected will likely shake our confidence.

A City of "Southern Efficiency and Northern Charm"

Most presidents leave Washington, D.C., with, at best, mixed feelings about the place and the many people with whom they've worked—especially the press. Perhaps that is why so many choose never to live there after leaving office and visit infrequently.

John F. Kennedy once called Washington a city of "Southern efficiency and Northern charm."

Harry Truman famously said that if you want a friend in Washington, "get a dog."

Martin Van Buren summed up how many presidents feel when he said, "The two happiest days of my life were those of my entrance upon the office and my surrender of it."

The adulation and thrills of a winning campaign soon give way to what Thomas Jefferson called the "drudgery" of a "nauseating and intolerable" city. Sure enough, for presidents, Washington is full of conniving wannabes, untrustworthy sycophants, and utterly annoying reporters. The reliably blunt Truman referred to the press corps as "guttersnipes" and "character assassins."

After Jimmy Carter left office he received one of the White House reporters who had once covered him and played a telling joke with his computer. Showing off his new machine, Carter typed the reporter's name and then hit the delete button.

"See, I can delete you," he said with a grin.

Ah, if it were only that easy, Mr. President.

"The Past Sharpens Perspective"

Dealing with a tough-to-please electorate and keeping your sanity, your integrity, and your ability to lead is what makes great presidents. There is much to learn from their experiences.

Those who succumb to bitterness, jealousy, and vindictiveness usually fail. There is much to learn from them too.

Every president ought to be an expert historian, well studied in the successes and failures of his predecessors. Dwight Eisenhower said, "The past sharpens perspective, warns of pitfalls, and helps to point the way."

It would be helpful for voters to learn more about past presidents. Comparing and contrasting candidates for the Oval Office to the best and worst in history is useful for voters who don't want to repeat past mistakes and want to make the right choice for the times. It might not be realistic to expect voters to work that hard, but citizenship in a democracy works best when voters know enough about the past to build a better future.

Voters should also observe the current campaign. How presidential candidates run for office is worth close examination. How they manage a campaign is often how they will govern. Barack Obama, for example, presided over one of the most efficient campaign organizations in history. There is a quiet competence about the man that voters found reassuring. One of Obama's secrets was that he had no tolerance for infighting among aides—a policy that Ronald Reagan followed to great effect. It's a management technique that tends to discourage news leaks. (The news media prefer infighting. Feuding aides tattling on each other is often how we get a story.)

Richard Nixon ran a reckless reelection campaign in 1972 that depended on dirty tricks and corrupt financing. How funny that the abbreviated name for his election committee was CREEP. Although he won in a landslide, the criminality of his campaign foreshadowed illegality in his White House.

Understanding a candidate's character is also important for evaluating how he will manage the pressures of office. What type of person typically seeks the job? While every president is a unique individual, there are some characteristics most have in common— and which sometimes cause them trouble.

For starters, most presidents like to hear themselves talk. (Teddy Roosevelt probably made it worse by calling the office a "bully pulpit.") But they don't like to be questioned, especially by the news media. George W. Bush refused to take follow-up questions at press conferences. It's much easier to stick to your talking points if you don't let anyone probe your answers.

While being a good talker helps you communicate with the public, Mr. President, being a good listener can help you manage the hardest job in the world. Presidents tend not to be good listeners. The massive ego required to win office tends to get in the way. Yet the advantage in learning to be a better listener is that it might just lead to better decisions. Stubborn overconfidence that shuts out alternative thinking will sometimes make your problems worse. Listening to wise counsel before making decisions will help you avoid the stress that comes with the fallout from a bad decision. So know your limits and take good advice, Mr. President.

Most presidents are true extroverts, feeding off the energy of a crowd. One major exception was Calvin Coolidge, who was so laid back and shy that the writer Dorothy Parker, when told of his death, said, "How can you tell?"

While we might debate whether Coolidge was a good president, one thing seems sure: He didn't let the job get to him. Some Coolidge-like calm is probably a good model for presidents under a lot of stress.

Know Your Faults

While it is abundantly obvious that presidents are human beings, too often we expect from them perfect behavior that mere mortals cannot achieve.

Keeping secrets about their personal imperfections is a passion for typical presidents. Ronald Reagan once joked, "There are advantages to being elected president—the day after I was elected, I had my high school grades classified Top Secret."

While you are president, bad behavior should be kept in check because chances are that you will not be able to keep it a secret. There are simply too many people watching to ever think you won't get caught. Bill Clinton's thinking that he could conduct a sexual affair in the modern age of Internet gossip and not get caught was about the dumbest move ever. In the old days his affair might simply have been fodder for private gossip. But websites such as the Drudge Report were most eager to make it a public spectacle.

Richard Nixon's personal insecurities were positively Shakespearean. He was undone in large part by an inability to recognize and contain his paranoia about perceived enemies. This fault, along with his jealousy of political figures such as John F. Kennedy, compounded the woes of office for him.

Our only president to resign from office, Nixon achieved great things—chief among them opening the diplomatic door to China—but was undermined by pathologies that only the Bard himself could have scripted.

In Hollywood director Oliver Stone's mostly factual film *Nixon,* British actor Anthony Hopkins portrays the delusional president wandering around the White House after hours talking to the portraits of other presidents. In one imaginary scene, he addresses his political nemesis, John F. Kennedy, with lines that not only sum up Nixon's destructive jealousy, but also describe the difficult balancing act for presidents whose predecessor leaves a positive legacy.

"They look at you and see who they want to be," Stone's "Nixon" says. "They look at me and see who they are." While the scene was fictional, the sentiment was real.

Above Us, Yet Among Us

Great presidents tend to be those who inspire by being who Americans aspire to be, while also seeming to be one of the people. The presidency is an exalted position, to be sure, but getting too used to the high altitude of that lofty pedestal can ensure that one day you will be knocked down from it.

One of our most popular and successful presidents, Franklin D. Roosevelt, was raised in wealthy privilege far beyond anything average Americans could imagine, then or now. And yet most citizens believed he truly understood their concerns thanks to an uncanny knack for speaking their language. Historians speculate that Roosevelt partly learned this skill in Warm Springs, Georgia, where, to the horror of his rich family, he chose to recuperate from his crippling polio, trying to learn to walk again surrounded by lower-class and rural people.

In a letter to his wife, Eleanor, from Warm Springs, FDR wrote of his awakening to the plight of poor people that "rattles my soul." In a fitting completion of the unique circle of his life, Roosevelt died there at the end of one of the greatest presidencies in American history.

Ronald Reagan was another widely popular president with a common touch despite a glamorous life as a Hollywood actor. In his case, Reagan's simpatico with average Americans stemmed from a typically middle-class upbringing in Illinois.

Voters should not overdo demanding the common touch if it comes with a lack of other important skills. It is often said during campaigns that a winning candidate is the one with whom most voters would "want to have a beer," the down-to-earth person who seems most like the rest of us. Putting aside the fact that few Americans will ever get such a chance, going too far with such an average standard would mean that we'd end up with a lot of mediocre presidents.

After all, it is unlikely that the average American would make a good president.

Being above us, and yet one of us, is perhaps your toughest challenge, Mr. President, and failing to meet it is a big reason so many of your predecessors left office in shame or regret.

"You Are the One in Trouble Now"

Remaining keenly aware of the struggles and troubles ahead, without being consumed by them, should keep you grounded in reality, Mr. President. It might even help you avoid getting blindsided by a crisis that you could have seen coming.

Many presidents learn the hard way just how demanding and difficult the job can be. It can be so awful that you have to wonder why dozens of seemingly sane people run for the job every four years. More than a few who actually won the office at times pondered whether it was worth it.

At the outset of what would be a grueling twenty-two-month campaign to become the nation's forty-fourth president, Barack Obama seemed unsure to aides. Some wondered if he really wanted it bad enough when the Illinois senator asked what sounded like a naïve question.

"Will I be able to take weekends off?" the Democrat pondered aloud. Obama soon learned that presidential candidates—and especially presidents—get precious few weekend furloughs.

Vice presidents who unexpectedly ascended to the presidency without the long campaigns that prepare one for the rigors of office soon became acutely aware of what they inherited.

On April 12, 1945, the day President Roosevelt passed away, his vice president, Harry S. Truman, remarked to reporters, "Pray for me, boys, the moon and the stars just fell on me."

Those in Truman's situation often provoked pity from those who really knew what they were in for. Also on that fateful day in 1945, FDR's grieving widow demonstrated that she felt even sorrier for what awaited the man who would succeed him.

Truman was a bit stunned by the reaction he got from First Lady Eleanor Roosevelt as he offered consolation. "Is there anything I can do for you?" Truman asked.

Without a pause, Mrs. Roosevelt brushed aside Truman's concern, saying, "Is there anything we can do for you? For you are the one in trouble now."

It wasn't so much that Mrs. Roosevelt felt the times were especially tough for the new president. World War II was winding down and the nation's economy was on the upswing. She was really referring to the pressures of a job that is overwhelming in the best of times.

Just a week or so after that initial exchange, Mrs. Roosevelt sent a handwritten letter to Truman expanding upon her warning. Enclosing one her husband's favorite figurines, a comical-looking donkey, Mrs. Roosevelt wrote, "This little donkey has long been in my husband's possession and was on his desk. He looks a bit obstinate and Franklin said he needed a reminder sometimes that his decisions had to be final and taken with a sense that God would give guidance to a humble beast. Once having decided something, the obstinate little donkey kept his sense of humor and determination going against great pressure."

Truman wrote back about the donkey, "He certainly is in a typical mulish attitude and, as the President used to say, when I have a hard decision to make I will look at him, think of you and the President, and then try to make the best decision."

Mrs. Roosevelt's early thoughts about Truman's needs apply to all new presidents.

You are still a "humble beast," Mr. President, just a human being who will make mistakes. You will face great pressure and will very much need to keep a sense of humor.

Find Advisers Worth Trusting

There is also a lesson for new presidents in how Truman nourished a warm and lasting friendship with Mrs. Roosevelt. During FDR's presidency the two had kept their distance. They were from different regions and factions of the Democratic Party. Their relationship was formal and wary during Franklin's life.

But what arose from that fateful day in 1945 was a warm friendship, full of frequent correspondence that allowed Truman to grow in office with the help of someone who had truly been there. Ultimately, Truman rewarded Eleanor Roosevelt's valued counsel by designating her as his representative to the United Nations, dubbing her "First Lady of the World."

Mr. President, look for the Eleanor Roosevelts in your world—trustworthy souls who've been there and understand the universal pressures of such a lonely job. They might even be former presidents or White House aides from an opposing party.

A few such relationships can help a new president manage everything from the mundane, such as how to keep your wits about you in the White House fishbowl, to weightier matters, like dealing with a particularly difficult member of Congress or another world leader.

Find a Management Style That Works for You

When it comes to constitutional tools for making a difference, especially on domestic matters, the president is not nearly as powerful as most Americans think—and certainly not as powerful as presidential candidates make it sound when they make promises on the campaign trail.

The almost inevitable failure to meet unreasonable expectations is often what makes a president miserable. Effective management can make even the worst times a little better.

Some presidents cope with the stress by delegating more than they should. Setting your administration's priorities is often a matter of demonstrating to aides and cabinet members just how much you are interested in a particular matter. Showing you care stirs the pot, and it can be done without micromanaging.

Other presidents aggravate their stress by getting too involved. Jimmy Carter probably lost reelection in 1980 largely because he and his entire White House got completely sidetracked into a long-running obsession with the Iranian hostage crisis. The imprisonment of American diplomats and staff at our own embassy in Tehran became a national obsession because the president made it so, taking personal responsibility for every nuance and daily development.

As a result, his failure to retrieve the hostages became Carter's personal failure. In addition, the president's high-profile public handling of the matter served to elevate the status of the young, radical hostage takers among their supporters, providing a disincentive for them to resolve it. As long as the president was publicly talking about them every day, they had every reason to keep the crisis going and focus world attention on their cause.

Even on more mundane matters, Carter was well known for micromanaging, right down to the schedule of the White House tennis court. His intricately involved style is the mirror opposite of George W. Bush's laid-back approach. Future presidents ought to strive for something in between.

Finding that critical balance between being in charge and taking on too much is any new president's first and foremost management challenge.

Lower Expectations

It might serve the country well if we expected less and did not hold presidents accountable for everything from the price of milk to the ups and downs of the stock market. It would certainly make their job more manageable and tolerable if we only held them accountable for things they could actually control.

You ought to be careful about raising expectations, Mr. President. It will not be easy transitioning from the grand promises of a campaign, but you will be able to do a better job if you are open and honest, with yourself and the public, about the realities of what is and is not truly achievable.

But the ever-expanding ambitions of modern presidents have conditioned Americans to think they can do anything.

Most of the nation's founders, except mavericks like Alexander

Hamilton, never meant for the presidency to become the center of attention in our federal government, and certainly not the "be all and end all" of power that some presidents imagine for themselves. In fact, our first president, George Washington, occasionally preferred the less noble and commonly used title of "chief magistrate," describing himself that way in his second inaugural address.

Congress was supposed to be the center of attention and power. Perhaps that is why the Constitution's authors started with detailing the powers of the legislative branch under Article I. The executive branch came second. Some delegates to the Constitutional Convention in 1787 even wanted Congress to choose presidents, to ensure that they would serve only at the pleasure of the legislative branch.

Until the mid-twentieth century, presidents more or less kept to their modest place as described in the Constitution. After World War II, however, the nation's new status as global superpower transformed the president into what became known as "leader of the free world."

What a far cry that is from "chief magistrate." And yet the "leader of the free world" must still operate under a Constitution that was written for a time when presidents were second-rate powers compared to the role envisioned for Congress.

The President Proposes, Congress Disposes

Over time, presidents have almost written a new Constitution for themselves, broadening their reach in ways unimagined by the founding fathers. Congress, often bullied by a popular president's public support, has gradually given away many of its written powers, such as its exclusive constitutional right to declare war.

Technically, presidents cannot introduce legislation in Congress, but now we expect them to present their own agenda, and we measure their effectiveness by how successfully they steer bills through the House and Senate. (FDR popularized the notion that presidents must introduce and pass ambitious legislative initiatives in their first hundred days in office.)

Still, many presidents have learned the hard way that Congress sometimes remembers to assert its powers. As the saying goes, "The President proposes, while Congress disposes."

The seemingly endless cajoling of lawmakers is a major cause of presidential stress and disappointment. Bullying Congress is another one of those powers, Mr. President, that is much easier on the day you're inaugurated than in the last days of your tenure.

Know Your Real Mandate

Carefully define the popular mandate of your election and you can use it as a battering ram on Capitol Hill. Politicians typically fear the voters. Convince them that your programs are what the voters elected you to pursue, and then, for a time, Congress will follow.

Know what you were elected to do, Mr. President, and be careful about overstating it—you and your party will be punished if you exceed your mandate. Press hard and fast for the things you promised—you will likely never have so much political capital as when you first take office. Political strength must be spent or it will be lost as time goes by.

Be aware of those who would sidetrack you. During the early days of his first term, President Clinton became embroiled in a national debate over gays in the military, a fight he never meant to start—at least not so soon.

Although relaxing rules against gays serving in uniform was on Clinton's long-term to-do list, it was his political enemies who made it appear that it was at the top of the list. They even provoked the Joint Chiefs of Staff to grumble. This drew Clinton into defending the idea or risk angering those in his liberal base who expected him to do so.

Eventually, Clinton reached a compromise that made neither side very happy, and encouraged conservatives in Congress to stand up to him on other issues, such as his ultimately unsuccessful efforts to expand health insurance to all Americans.

Clinton's experience, and that of many other new presidents, demonstrates how Washington manipulators can get the best of a new and popular president by detouring his agenda to something that most voters did not consider to be his major focus.

Play the Veto Card

Use your veto power, Mr. President, if you want to beat the stress of dealing with a recalcitrant Congress. That is certainly a lesson from the last hundred years of U.S. history.

The veto has become a symbol of presidential power over Congress even though it is not a specific act under the Constitution, which uses passive language to describe this power. The word "veto" does not even appear in the document.

Bills that pass Congress are to be presented to the president for signature. If the legislation is not approved—a rare occurrence as the nation's founders envisioned this power—the Constitution calls for its return to Congress for reconsideration and the opportunity to override the president's disapproval by a two-thirds majority.

The history of the presidential veto demonstrates how it became a powerful tool in the last half of the nation's history. Used sparingly until the late 1800s (the nation's first twenty-one presidents issued a grand total of 205 vetoes), it gradually grew to play a vital role in presidential dominance over the legislative branch. The next twenty-two presidents dramatically upped the ante with 2,352 vetoes.

Congress has proven to be rather weak in the face of the modern presidency's veto binge, overriding only 6 percent during the past century.

Beware Your War Powers

The greatest expansion of presidential power is rooted in the Constitution's most significant grant of authority to the chief executive: command of the military.

Presidents in the last century or more have broadened their role as commander in chief from running wars to starting them.

Declaring war was strictly supposed to be in the hands of Congress. No longer. Thanks to Capitol Hill's repeated silence or cooperation in the face of presidential initiatives, this constitutional mandate is all but gone.

Be careful on this front, Mr. President. Even though your predecessors have established your extra-constitutional authority to send Americans to their death without a congressional declaration of war, many were ultimately undone by using it.

Lyndon Baines Johnson's otherwise remarkable achievements on the domestic front were, in the short term at least, almost forgotten in the great tragedy of the Vietnam War. Had he been forced to listen to those in Congress who opposed escalation, Johnson might not have abused the presidency's war-making powers to such an extent that he was ultimately powerless to run for reelection.

Johnson's expansive view of his authority and office as his private preserve were comically revealed one day on the South Lawn of the White House as a phalanx of helicopters assembled to transport his entourage.

"Mr. President, which helicopter is yours?" someone asked.

"Son, they're all mine," Johnson replied.

Ronald Reagan nearly got impeached because of his own administration's unrestrained ideas about presidential clout in foreign conflicts. When Congress refused to fund Reagan's desire to fight communist leaders in Nicaragua, his White House embarked upon one of the most aggressive efforts to circumvent legislators. They turned to foreign sources for the money that Congress wouldn't appropriate, including a clandestine program to sell weapons to Iran to raise the money.

The so-called Iran-Contra affair forced Reagan to fire aides and fess up to the scheme or face impeachment—severely weakening his presidency.

Although Reagan narrowly escaped personal harm with a nationally televised address acknowledging his administration's overreaching, his vice president and successor, George H. W. Bush, ultimately paid the price.

The elder Bush's reelection drive in 1992 was derailed partly by election-eve federal indictments of former Reagan officials in the Iran-Contra matter. Although Bush's personal involvement in the scandal was never made entirely clear, voters seemed to hold him accountable.

Bush's son George W. Bush also suffered the loss of public support on the heels of his exercise of assumed presidential war powers. Congress authorized Bush's 2003 invasion of Iraq without ever formally declaring war, which made it his war. Bush was in fine shape so long as the public agreed with his action, but when the Iraq War became unpopular it was *his* hide that was nailed to the wall.

Mr. President, you will be tempted to make unilateral choices that the expanded powers of your office now offer in foreign conflicts, thanks to the loose interpretations of the Constitution that allow it. But the lessons of most presidents who've done so suggest that you will be better off in the long run by making sure that Congress is on the hook. Just know that while you might be able to ram a war through Congress, if your war becomes unpopular, you could still get all the blame if lawmakers on Capitol Hill have successfully distanced themselves from what you've done.

Given the aggravating limits on presidential power in domestic matters, it might be a relief to be able to make your own decisions on committing troops abroad. Playing the role of commander in chief, protecting the national interest when Congress won't, is heady stuff, and the public might love you for it at first. Just remember the soured examples of Johnson, Reagan, and both Bushes before going too far with your war.

Accept the Limits to Your Power

Even today, after a long line of presidents who exploited every constitutional loophole so as to expand their power, there are still limits. Despite being chief executive of a government with around 4 million employees, presidents can hire and fire fewer than fifteen thousand.

That leaves millions of your own workers, Mr. President, who might not be waking up every morning to do your bidding. Plenty of them might even be political foes actively trying to undermine you.

You will be tempted toward paranoia as you realize how many government employees cannot be trusted. Leaks to the news media will infuriate you. It was Nixon's obsession with leaks that led to the formation of the so-called White House plumbers, the clandestine unit of unsavory characters charged with targeting the president's enemies, which included breaking into the Democratic National Committee headquarters at the Watergate office building in Washington. (In the end, it was Nixon's own "plumbers" who brought him down, not his enemies.)

Guard Against the Physical Toll

With so many potentially debilitating exceptions to what is essentially the illusion of supremacy, it is no wonder that presidents suffer physical wear and tear unlike that produced by just about any other job on the planet.

Woodrow Wilson, who ended his days in the White House as a reclusive invalid, once remarked, "Men of ordinary physique and discretion cannot be Presidents and live, if the strain cannot be somehow relieved. We shall be obliged to always be picking our chief magistrates from among wise and prudent athletes, a small class."

Even a president like Abraham Lincoln, who, as a young man, could literally chop wood faster than nearly any man around, was physically ravaged by the pressures of the office. Of course, Lincoln is the only president who faced the burdens of a Civil War that literally tore the nation apart. And as if that weren't enough, he dealt with personal tragedies, including the loss of a son as well as a wife who was mentally unstable.

During the course of his presidency, Lincoln lost thirty-five pounds—and he was no heavyweight when first elected! Thanks to the rather macabre practice in Lincoln's time of using plaster to make so-called life masks of famous or well-to-do people, we can see the incredible toll of his presidency by comparing the masks made at the beginning and end of his years in office. Of course, historians and scientists now suggest that he was dying of a rare genetic disease at the time of his assassination.

From a youngish face with smooth skin and strong cheekbones, Lincoln's plaster masks at the National Portrait Gallery in Washington, D.C., show how his face dramatically morphed into the sagging skin and deep lines of someone who seemed to have aged by twenty or thirty years instead of less than a decade.

Of course, no other president had to preside over such a deadly war as Lincoln did. But plenty of others faced miserable times, and aged accordingly.

Truman famously said of his job that "the buck stops here." Presidents are the last stop in a vast pipeline of decision making. The toughest choices end up on the Oval Office desk, the ones that underlings can't or won't decide.

Like all people, presidents need diversion from the drudgery of work. Do not neglect this need, Mr. President.

Presidential pastimes run the gamut, but Obama was the first to add basketball to the list of favorite things chief executives do to get away from it all.

"I could play basketball with a consuming passion that would always exceed my limited talent," Obama modestly wrote in his memoir.

Obama gets more credit from those who've been on the court with the former high school basketball player.

"He has a very nice outside shot that has gotten better over the years," Obama's brother-in-law, Craig Robinson, wrote in *Time* magazine. "He's thin, but he's not weak. You can tell the guy has played." Robinson wrote that basketball is "very therapeutic" for Obama, that "he's always in a good mood before and after he's played."

Harry Truman and Richard Nixon played the piano. Nixon also liked to bowl. A workaholic, Nixon once remarked that he liked bowling because "it doesn't take up much time."

If you are going to have a pastime that does any good, Mr. President—and you should—shouldn't it take some time? Who knows, if Nixon was as serious about his pastimes as he was about his enemies, perhaps he would not have lost his presidency.

Herbert Hoover once joked about fishing as his only refuge from the prying eyes of the public and the press.

"Fishing is the only labor or recreation open to a president in which both the press and the public are prepared to concede privacy," Hoover said in a speech to journalists at Washington's annual Gridiron Club dinner. "Next to prayer, fishing is the most personal relationship of man. Everyone concedes that fish will not bite in the presence of the representatives of the press. Fishing is thus the sole avenue now left to a public man that he may escape to his own thoughts, may live in his own imaginings."

Go for a Walk

Harry Truman enjoyed a quite simple daily pastime that any president can emulate. He liked to walk. He deeply believed in it as a stress buster and an exercise regimen.

"As part of my daily routine, I usually take a walk of a mile and a half, at a pace of 120 steps a minute," Truman said. "If you walk 120 paces a minute, your whole body gets a vigorous workout. You swing your arms and take deep breaths as you walk. After you are fifty years old, this is the best exercise you can get. Some aging exhibitionists try to prove that they can play tennis or handball or anything else. And every once in a while one of them falls dead of a heart attack. I say that's not for me."

In 1948, shortly after winning reelection, back in his hometown of Independence, Missouri, he formed the Truman Early Risers Walking Society. It was populated mostly by journalists and photographers who could keep up with him on his brisk walks before breakfast.

Routine walks might be a good idea, Mr. President. Truman lived to see his eighty-eighth birthday.

Truman chose a modest cottage at the Key West Naval Station in Florida for his favorite getaway spot. He sat in the sun wearing colorful shirts and played lots of poker at night. He ended up spending 175 days there during his nearly eight years in office.

"I am getting some much needed rest and already feel and look much better," Truman wrote to his wife, Bess, during a 1947 trip to Key West. "Have been going to bed at eleven o'clock and getting up at seven or eight, so you see I am really doing some sleeping."

John Quincy Adams and Teddy Roosevelt were fond of skinny-dipping. According to a popular story in Adams's day, the president was out for a predawn swim in the Potomac River when a female reporter decided it was a prime opportunity for an unexpected interview. She sat on his clothes by the bank, forcing the president to answer her questions.

Golf has been a popular hobby for many presidents. William Howard Taft was the first. He thought it might be an effective way to lose weight. But it did not make a dent in his three-hundred-pound girth. Woodrow Wilson was our most dedicated golfer, although Gerald Ford was the most skilled.

Wilson is thought to hold the record for the most golf played by a president. He reportedly logged more than a thousand rounds during his presidency, playing almost every other day. He was even determined to play in the snow during the winter, and the Secret Service painted his golf balls black so he could hit them around the White House lawn.

Franklin Roosevelt collected stamps. But unlike your average stamp collector, Roosevelt had special powers. While president, he took the liberty of designing stamps for the postal service.

Many presidents have been wealthy enough to own retreats where they could escape the pressures of office—and mostly disappear from public view.

Ronald Reagan loved his mountaintop ranch in California. He was probably the first president since Lincoln to chop wood for sport. He was always very careful to explain, for the sake of environmentalists, that he did not cut down trees for his chopping pleasure. Instead, he attacked already downed targets.

In an interview for the local newspaper, Reagan described why he liked to chop wood: "It's a real change. I think part of it also is that there's always a kick in building something. And we did a lot of work—all those wood fences that we put in that weren't there, a lot of work on the house itself. It was a little, old adobe that was built in 1872, and we did most of the work ourselves there, fixing it up—the fences. You get a good feeling out of what you've accomplished there."

George H. W. Bush preferred his family's longtime retreat in Maine, where he particularly enjoyed buzzing the waters around Kennebunkport in his flashy speedboat. Usually a frenetic vacationer, on at least one occasion Bush decided to slow things down a bit and went fishing in his snazzy vessel, a so-called cigarette boat. With the motor purring at low speed, the president's boat inched near shore where a man and his grandson were casting their fishing poles.

The man looked up at the somewhat ridiculous sight of Bush trolling for fish in a speedboat and shouted to the president. "Only in America," he said.

In a speech to sporting enthusiasts near his Kennebunkport home, Bush struck a note of humorous defiance about his determination to get away from the White House.

"As your President, I will not ever miss any opportunity at all to go fishing, to go hiking, to go camping, to go out in my boat. I want to do my part. And so, I'll go to work early in the morning and sometimes go home late at night. I'll be damned if I'm going to let anybody keep me from the great outdoors."

Laugh More and You'll Cry Less

As for any difficult occupation, a sense of humor goes a long way toward coping with stress.

It has always seemed that presidents with a sense of humor make happier presidents—and citizens too. It's not that you have to be a world-class joke teller, like Ronald Reagan, or a master of the witty retort, like John Kennedy.

Lighten up, Mr. President, whenever you can. There are plenty of reasons in a job like yours to mope around like the weight of the world is on your shoulders—because it is. Still, that doesn't mean you can't enjoy yourself on occasion.

Sometimes it's enough to simply enjoy having humorous people around you, or be a good sport about being the butt of a joke now and then. Just playing the straight man, as comics call it, can help humanize presidents and ease their own tension.

A reporter once got the bigger laugh when Lyndon Johnson tried to have some fun. He had invited scholars, with the press in tow, to tour the Lincoln Bedroom in the White House.

Johnson turned to Wauhillau LaHay, a Scripps-Howard reporter in her fifties, and said, "Bet you've never been in a president's bedroom?"

"Not since Millard Fillmore," she replied.

Sure, hardly the knee slapper of a *Saturday Night Live* skit. But the lighter moments between presidents and those they deal with help remind them and their subjects that we're all human beings doing the best we can. We're not talking here about hiring joke writers to help you deliver comedy when it's called for. That is sometimes part of the job, such as when presidents are expected to be funny at the White House Correspondents Association dinners. It's important to do that, but often that is just more pressure on you to perform for an audience.

Nurturing a sense of irony and wit about the surreal life you lead will improve your mood in the worst of times. Kennedy enjoyed teasing those around him, especially at difficult moments. When women reporters were protesting at the National Press Club because, in those days, only men were allowed in, Kennedy defused the moment as he entered the club to give a speech.

"There's one of the troublemakers," he said, pointing to one of the female journalist-protesters.

"We forgive you officially, but not personally," she said.

Presidents have displayed all types of humor. Whatever works for you is the way to go. Lincoln and Reagan loved to tell long stories with hilarious punch lines. In both cases they were sometimes able to disarm opponents in private meetings or delight the public in ways that made them seem more human.

For humor at a truly awful moment, it is tough to beat Ronald Reagan on the day in 1981 when he was shot in an assassination attempt.

"Honey, I forgot to duck," the badly injured Reagan said to a distraught Nancy Reagan as she rushed into his hospital room. We learned he was quoting the words of boxer Jack Dempsey to his wife after he lost to Gene Tunney in 1926.

As doctors prepared Reagan for surgery, he managed another zinger with the famous line, "I hope you're all Republican." Dr. Joseph Giordano replied, "We're all Republicans today."

Such grace under the scalpel ought to be an inspiration to future presidents facing a tough challenge, whether personal or political.

Barack Obama seems to possess the droll wit of a Franklin Roosevelt, who once broke the tension of attacks on his administration by referring to his famous dog, a Scottish terrier named Fala.

"I do not mind the attacks on me," Roosevelt told an audience. "My family does not mind the attacks. . . . But Fala does mind."

It was the subject of a White House dog that lightened the mood at Obama's first press conference following his election in November of 2008. Obama mocked the same semi-serious tone that Roosevelt had adopted in referring to Fala.

Asked about the dog he had promised to get for his young daughters when moving into the White House, Obama ponderously, but humorously, answered in the same grave manner with which he had handled weighty questions about the troubled economy.

"With respect to the dog, this is a major issue," Obama said. "I think it's generated more interest on our website than just about anything. We have . . . we have two criteria that have to be reconciled. One is that Malia is allergic, so it has to be hypoallergenic. There are a number of breeds that are hypoallergenic. On the other hand, our preference would be to get a shelter dog, but, obviously, a lot of shelter dogs are mutts like me. So . . . so whether we're going to be able to balance those two things I think is a pressing issue on the Obama household."

Clearly not schooled in the Reagan-esque storytelling technique or particularly facile with a Kennedy-like quick comeback, Obama seems to enjoy a more quaint sense of humor that spotlights the irony of silly questions or bizarre moments.

Whatever works for you, Mr. President, get a laugh whenever you can. Laughs are hard to come by in this job.

TWO

YOU ARE NOT ABOVE THE LAW:
READ THE CONSTITUTION

A dictatorship would be a heck of a lot easier.
—PRESIDENT GEORGE W. BUSH

Mr. President, your best job description is right there in the Constitution—the Oath of Office.

"I do solemnly swear (or affirm) that I will faithfully execute the Office of President of the United States, and will to the best of my ability, preserve, protect and defend the Constitution of the United States."

If you really do what it says—preserve, protect, and defend the Constitution—you are doing your job. Anything less and you're a failure, or worse. Not meeting this standard could, and probably should—get you impeached and thrown out of office.

As president, you should govern within the constitutional boundaries you're given. Trying to reinterpret those boundaries to expand your power might "preserve, protect, and defend" yourself and your office, but that is not what you swore to do on Inauguration Day.

Constitutionally, using your power can be tricky, to be sure. For that you need to choose a model for your governing style, one that is flexible enough for adapting to different circumstances but clear enough, at least in your own mind, to guide you and your staff in getting important things done despite the institutional and constitutional limits.

New presidents should think long and hard about developing a guiding theory for how they govern to avoid the chaos and unpopularity that ensues without it.

Choose Your Model

Presidential scholar James MacGregor Burns has written extensively about three basic categories for presidential governing. Presidents generally fall under one of three models (even though they might occasionally deploy the others in certain circumstances):

- Madisonian Model: A principal architect of the Constitution, James Madison was faithful to the document's intent that the president rely on Congress to lead in setting policy. The president mainly administers policies set by Congress.
- Hamiltonian Model: Alexander Hamilton, also a constitutional author, held a very different view from Madison's. The president should be heroic and above partisanship, relying on public opinion for support and ignoring Congress if necessary.
- Jeffersonian Model: Thomas Jefferson's approach to the presidency relied on the support of his political party. His model would have the president act in similar ways to a prime minister in a parliamentary system. The party, influenced and led by the president, sets policy. The president assists the party with getting its members' platform enacted.

Madisonian presidents tend to be incremental managers who do not leave much of a legacy for the history books, which is probably why modern occupants of the White House steer clear of the Congress-first example, even if that is more faithful to what the Constitution intended.

Historians consider William Howard Taft probably our last Madisonian president. More of a legal technician than a skilled political actor, Taft approached governing like a Swiss watch, working the levers of our system of checks and balances with precision. Still, he was not one to sit and wait for congressional authority to execute his powers. Taft got quite a bit done, such as instituting the income tax, expanding civil service, strengthening the Interstate Commerce Commission, and significantly improving the postal system.

Jeffersonian presidents like Woodrow Wilson got much done by expertly using their role as party leaders to steer Congress, but in the end these powers failed him in his vain efforts to create a League of Nations—so much so that he suffered a debilitating stroke while barnstorming the country to campaign for it.

Wilson was such an admirer of Jeffersonian-style party rule that early in his political career he advocated a change to the Constitution to create a parliamentary-style government, replacing popularly elected presidents with a prime minister chosen by the majority party in Congress. By the time he was president, however, Wilson had changed his mind. Eventually, he came around to the prevailing view, more or less defining the modern presidency by saying that it "will be as big as and as influential as the man who occupies it."

Heroic presidents of the Hamiltonian type are now the norm, although the overreaching and power-grabbing that often comes with this style causes some to end up as villains to many Americans. We now look to them for leadership and results beyond anything the job was actually created to achieve.

The two Roosevelts, Theodore and Franklin, and John F. Kennedy set the Hamiltonian model in stone. Their inspirational eloquence and charismatic personalities produced a power base of popular appeal that at times made Congress seem almost irrelevant to most citizens—even if it wasn't.

You Cannot Hide When You Break the Law

Instead of accepting the frustrations that go with the hard work of choosing a model for maximizing power within legal limits, deciding to do an end run around those limits is a dangerous choice.

Nixon's tragic demise should be a lesson to his successors forevermore. You are not above the law, Mr. President. Do not forget it.

There was a frightening moment for the press corps at the end of Nixon's presidency. It came at a time of speculation about whether the president would finally step down or take more extreme measures to stay in power.

They locked the press room doors at the White House that day in 1974 when, as it turned out, Nixon went on his last walk around the South Lawn. Reporters were trapped inside, unable to go watch these final hours before Nixon became the first president to resign from office.

This press "lockdown" was unprecedented and a bit frightening for press locked inside the White House press room. Reporters called their offices for help, but no one was even allowed inside. For all they knew, something terrible had happened. It was, instead, the final desperate act of an administration determined to hide.

Holding reporters hostage was a fitting end, perhaps, to such an outlaw presidency. It was, after all, the press that exposed the wrong-doing that brought him down.

The crimes of Nixon's "Watergate" scandal are legion, ranging from third-rate burglaries to the president himself obstructing justice. Ultimately, Congress asserted its constitutional powers to seek Nixon's impeachment and, rather than stand trial in the Senate, he resigned.

Presidents tend to think that some laws do not apply to them. Often they cite national security as their justification, calling it "emergency powers." Other times they assert "executive privilege" to protect themselves and their staffs from scrutiny.

On some occasions they simply believe that presidents are above reproach for matters that have nothing to do with their duties, as when Bill Clinton chose to lie about his sexual involvement with a White House intern.

Whether it involves great matters of state or protecting themselves from personal embarrassment, presidents too often believe they are above the law. The fact that they are not is a hallmark of our democracy, and despite the painful turmoil sometimes caused by bringing presidents back to earth, doing so is a healthy reminder that we are a nation of laws, not men.

Too Cute by Signing

Presidents can be quite creative about trying to place themselves beyond the law's reach—even before a law becomes law. So-called signing statements are now in vogue for presidents wishing to keep their options open. When signing an enacted bill into law, they add a statement detailing parts of it that they might choose not to enforce.

But the Constitution says nothing about a president issuing any statement when he signs a bill into law. If he vetoes the bill, the Constitution requires him to tell Congress what his objections are so that Congress can reconsider the bill and accommodate him or pass it again with a two-thirds vote in the House and Senate, enacting the law without his signature.

President Barack Obama vowed to slow down the practice, compared to his recent predecessors, but issued his first signing statement within the first two months of taking office. Although his objections were aimed at minor parts of a massive spending bill, Obama's signing statement echoed those of the recent past by indicating—with phrases such as, "I do not interpret this provision to detract from my authority in cases where such communications would be unlawful," or "These are impermissible forms of legislative aggrandizement"— that he would not implement laws that he believed would undermine his authority.

He also deployed another device common to modern signing statements, referring to one congressional mandate as something he would treat "as advisory" only.

These attempts to modify the meaning of laws are not authorized anywhere in the Constitution. The American Bar Association (ABA) has described signing statements as "contrary to the rule of law and our constitutional system of separation of powers." The Supreme Court has shown some dislike for the practice, but has not yet squarely addressed the issue.

George W. Bush significantly stepped up the use of signing statements. Until his time in office, all previous presidents combined produced fewer than six hundred challenges to the bills they signed. Bush issued more than eight hundred by himself. In one, he famously used a signing statement to block congressional oversight of the war in Iraq.

Not only did Bush increase the quantity of signing statements, he also enhanced their quality as tools for expanding presidential power. He did so with a momentous change in wording, according to political science professor John T. Woolley of the University of California's American Presidency Project (americanpresidency.org). "Basically, Bush asserted that Congress cannot pass a law that undercuts the constitutionally granted authorities of the President," Woolley wrote.

This language asserts a presidential prerogative to declare laws, or certain parts of them, unconstitutional even if he signs them into law. Presidents who add such statements when signing a bill are essentially saying that "some part of the legislation is unconstitutional and therefore they intend to ignore it or to implement it only in ways they believe is constitutional," according to Woolley.

In one frequently used phrase for his signing statements, Bush routinely asserted that he would not act contrary to the constitutional provisions that direct the president to "supervise the unitary executive branch." This formulation was first used in a signing statement of Ronald Reagan's, and was repeated several times by Bush. Before Bush, most presidential signing statements were less provocative.

Woolley and the researchers at the American Presidency Project found several sources that trace the emergence of signing statements back to James Monroe. Other statements that include discussions on presidential doubt about legislation and the issue of how the president should proceed are found from Andrew Jackson, John Tyler, James Polk, and Ulysses Grant.

The text of Monroe's first messages did not look like what are today considered signing statements. For instance, he informed Congress in a message on January 17, 1822, that he had resolved what he saw as a confusion in the law in a way that he thought was consistent with his constitutional authority. In other words, he was not trying to change the purpose of the law, but merely reconcile some contradictory language.

In 1830, Andrew Jackson wrote a message stating his understanding of the limits of an appropriation bill: "The phraseology of the section which appropriates the sum of $8,000 for the road from Detroit to Chicago may be construed to authorize the application of the appropriation for the continuance of the road beyond the limits of the Territory of Michigan. I desire to be understood as having approved this bill with the understanding that the road authorized by this section is not to be extended beyond the limits of the said Territory."

Again, a president was using this device simply to clear up a misunderstanding about language.

In response to one of John Tyler's signing statements expressing his view that a law might be unconstitutional, John Quincy Adams, who was then Speaker of the House, issued a harsh response. A future president himself, Adams wondered why such an "extraneous document" was issued at all and advised that the signing statement should "be regarded in no other light than a defacement of the public records and archives."

After the era of Jackson and Tyler, according to the American Bar Association study, the next round of presidents "seemed to shy away from statements denouncing provisions in bills they signed."

Ulysses Grant revived the tactic, issuing one statement that "interpreted" a bill in a way that would overcome his constitutional concern. That was still far short of refusing to enforce the law. This technique of interpreting laws to their liking would be used frequently by presidents throughout the twentieth century.

But as the power of the presidency grew in other areas, their signing statements grew bolder. Theodore Roosevelt proclaimed his intention in 1909 to ignore a restriction on his power to establish volunteer commissions. Woodrow Wilson advised in a signing statement that executing a particular provision would result in a violation of thirty-two treaties, and he refused to do so.

In 1943, Franklin Roosevelt vehemently lashed back at a rider in an appropriation bill that barred compensation to three government employees deemed "subversive" by the Congress. Roosevelt expressed his view that "this provision is not only unwise and discriminatory, but unconstitutional" and not binding on him. The Supreme Court later did hold the law unconstitutional.

Dwight Eisenhower introduced the practice of using signing statements to avoid intelligence disclosures. Nixon objected to a 1971 military authorization bill that set a date for the withdrawal of

U.S. forces from Vietnam as being "without binding force or effect." Jimmy Carter used them to resist congressional efforts to undermine some of his policies, such as his amnesty program for Vietnam draft resisters.

Reagan was the pioneer in upping the ante for presidential signing statements. The American Bar Association study notes that, under Reagan, "for the first time, signing statements were viewed as a strategic weapon in a campaign to influence the way legislation was interpreted by the courts and Executive agencies as well as their more traditional use to preserve Presidential prerogatives."

Although it might seem to be a minor formality, it was quite significant that Reagan's attorney general, Edwin Meese, secured an agreement from West Publishing Company to include signing statements along with traditional legislative history in the official United States Code. This made the presidential messages widely available to judges and other officials when interpreting the meaning of legislation.

Sure enough, some of Reagan's signing statements began showing up in judicial opinions, a major victory for legitimizing a presidential power that was not granted by the Constitution.

The number of such statements quickly grew in later administrations. Clinton became more aggressive in the reach of his statements once Republicans gained control of Congress in 1994.

But it was George W. Bush's aggressive signing statements—in wording and in their number—that represented the most historic leap forward in expanding presidential power.

The *Boston Globe* wrote that "the scope and aggression of Bush's assertions that he can bypass laws represent a concerted effort to expand his power at the expense of Congress, upsetting the balance between the branches of government."

"The President Must Accept the Limitations Imposed"

The ABA task force on signing statements, which included liberal and conservative scholars, could not have been more blunt.

"If our constitutional system of separation of powers is to operate as the framers intended, the President must accept the limitations imposed on his office by the Constitution itself," the task force wrote. "The use of presidential signing statements to have the last word as to which laws will be enforced and which will not is inconsistent with those limitations and poses a serious threat to the rule of law."

Not surprisingly, many veteran members of Congress are outraged. Senator Patrick Leahy (D-Vt.), a leader in Capitol Hill's struggle against signing statements, complains that presidents have taken "what was otherwise a press release and transformed it into a proclamation stating which parts of the law the President will follow and which parts he will simply ignore."

The proper presidential action when presented with legislation ought to be a simple up or down, either veto it (Constitution, Article I, section 7) or "faithfully execute" the law (Constitution, Article II, section 3). This burgeoning gray area of signing statements is something that future presidents could continue expanding until all laws mean whatever they say. That's dictatorship.

Still, there are legal scholars who defend the existence of signing statements while criticizing how they are done in some cases. In an essay for the *Boston Globe* in 2006, constitutional law professor Lawrence Tribe wrote that signing statements are "informative and constitutionally unobjectionable."

Tribe wrote that what is objectionable is when statements are used because of a "president's failure to face the political music by issuing a veto and subjecting that veto to the possibility of an override in Congress." An eventual challenge to a president should come not to the statement, Tribe wrote, but to the fact that a president failed to enforce a law or that his actions resulted in harm to others. Unless Congress or the courts push back, presidents are likely to make wide use of this tool for bending laws to their will.

Tribe has it right. Mr. President, if you don't want to enforce a law, veto it and send it back to Congress. Face the music.

The signing statement is one of many examples showing how presidents tend to think the Constitution means whatever suits them.

You are not a monarch, Mr. President. You have no birthright to power. You are an employee. Don't forget it.

Every president should well remember Nixon's path to disaster. Watergate was about petty crimes in the beginning, but the cover-up that brought him down was rooted in a president's belief that the law and the Constitution served him—and not the other way around, as it should be.

The presidential oath of office, after all, says the chief executive will "preserve, protect, and defend the Constitution." It does not say the Constitution exists to protect you and your power, Mr. President.

Even Your Dog Knows

Throughout 1974 there were many ominous signs of the impending downfall of Nixon's once imperial presidency, as one shoe fell after the other. Early in the year, Nixon could not even enjoy his own birthday without a mishap.

Nixon's staff tried to cheer up their dejected president by rolling a cake into his office at the western White House in San Clemente, California. With his Irish setter, King Timahoe, faithfully in tow, Nixon leaned over to read the inscription on the cake and got a bit too close. As he stood back up for the cameras, his face and jacket were smeared with icing.

There stood our president, cake icing and all, while a delighted King Timahoe licked some of it from his jacket. For once, stunned reporters in the room did not use this rare opportunity to toss him a question. To us it was proof that nothing could go right for him. There was nothing more to say.

Nixon's resignation stands as a virtual monument to setting limits on presidential overreaching. It is a lesson that presidents will probably have to learn again someday. The temptations to think that you're above the law can be too great to resist.

As a stern reminder of what can happen if you go too far, perhaps the Oval Office should permanently display the photo of Nixon waving to his staff from the helicopter doorstep before being whisked away on the day of his resignation. Either that photo or the one of his face smeared with cake icing.

Despite Nixon's fall, the history of our country is mostly about presidents getting away with power grabs that are either unconstitutional or of questionable legality. Often these assertions of new presidential authority are excused as legitimate "emergency powers" in a time of war or crisis.

Lincoln's Overreaching

Abraham Lincoln used his emergency powers to suspend the writ of habeas corpus—the right to seek relief for unlawful detention—during the Civil War. While the courts declared this unconstitutional, Lincoln simply ignored the order.

Once a president asserts a new emergency power, it tends to become law, even if opposed by Congress or the courts. George W. Bush's administration used Lincoln's example to indefinitely detain suspected foreign terrorists without trials. The courts tried to limit the president's efforts, but, like Lincoln, Bush did not pay much attention.

There is one of Lincoln's emergency actions that later presidents would probably like to repeat, but haven't. When a New York newspaper printed stories that Lincoln did not like, he composed an executive order in his own handwriting directing one of his generals to seize the newsroom, arrest the editors, and shut down the printing presses.

Let's hope that Lincoln will be the only president to ever do anything like that.

In a rare victory over the expansion of presidential emergency powers, the Supreme Court stopped Harry Truman's efforts to nationalize steel mills in an economic crisis.

Unfortunately, the public often enables presidents on a power binge. In a time of war or crisis, citizens are easily duped into allowing a president to do things they would never imagine permitting in normal times.

Mr. President, keep your sense of constitutional place even when you can politically get away with going beyond it. Some of the worst moments for even our greatest presidents were the product of thinking they could ignore human rights in a time of crisis. It was inexcusable that Franklin Roosevelt allowed the mass detention of Japanese-Americans during World War II. Even families with sons fighting for our country were in these camps.

Executive "Privilege" Is Not a Right

Executive privilege is a favorite tool for presidents who like to think that the chief executive is exempt from abiding by the law. The concept has no foundation in law, but generations of presidents have claimed it as a firewall against scrutiny, using it primarily to prevent congressional and official probes of questionable behavior. There is seldom any national purpose served in the exercise of executive privilege.

You might think that short-term needs require these constitutional lapses, Mr. President, but abusing these opportunities will become a scar on your legacy no matter how well your presidency is generally viewed.

No matter how high your poll ratings, you are not above the law. Even our most popular presidents can be brought down to earth when necessary.

Ronald Reagan's presidency was nearly undone by the Iran-Contra scandal. It took the intervention of his wife, the firing of top aides, and a televised presidential admission of wrongdoing to save Reagan from an impeachment ordeal.

The Iran-Contra affair was about as far as any president has gone to run a war around Congress. In most efforts of its kind, presidents at least get some sort of tacit approval for a military adventure, even if that permission slip is well short of the constitutional requirement that only Congress has the power to declare war.

Lyndon B. Johnson had his Gulf of Tonkin resolution. Although the truth of the actual events was murky, at best, hostilities against U.S. forces were used as a premise for Congress to permit an escalation of the Vietnam War.

In 2002, George W. Bush got his congressional authorization to invade Iraq. It was no declaration of war, but it did put Capitol Hill on the record favoring it once Bush chose to invade.

What was so remarkable about Reagan's persistence in fighting the Nicaragua communist government, with the Contra rebels as our proxy, was that Congress had specifically refused to authorize it or pay for it. The Reagan White House, however, undaunted by Congress or the Constitution, sought funding elsewhere, soliciting donations from foreign countries to pay for a war in Nicaragua. Several nations went along, all of it done in secret.

On top of that outrage, the Reagan team compounded its lawbreaking by secretly selling weapons to Iran despite a federal ban against it—and using the proceeds to support the Contras.

It took months of storming the stone walls around the White House—and endless congressional investigations—to finally get these truths out. And once the dust settled, the nation had to face the fact that this was one of the most egregious presidential power grabs in our history: an American president secretly conducting an illegal war with foreign funds. Naturally, a growing number of lawmakers on Capitol Hill were busily crafting articles of impeachment.

Damage Control Doesn't Have to Be a Cover-Up

The Reagan team's swift recognition of its political peril saved the day. Mr. President, here's a lesson. When the country figures out that your White House committed high crimes and misdemeanors, start firing people and get on television to fess up to the whole thing.

Thanks to First Lady Nancy Reagan's intensive behind-the-scenes efforts to replace her husband's management team, impeachment pressure began to wane on Capitol Hill. To finally put the issue to rest, the president had to go on national television to deliver a heart-felt mea culpa about the whole mess. In the end, the Reagans did everything they could to shift blame to underlings and assert that the president was somehow unaware of the full extent of the wrong-doing. Yet the American public, despite all the coverage and congres-sional testimony, never really got the full story.

Future presidents should always remember that even though Reagan is remembered as one of our most popular presidents, his presidency was very nearly undone by a massive breach of the Con-stitution.

At least two factors helped saved Reagan. First, the country was not in the mood for another impeachment ordeal so soon after Nixon's. And it was easier to believe Reagan's claims of ignorance. Still, it's dif-ficult to know what's worse: an administration running amok without the president's knowledge, or with his knowledge. The other contrib-uting factor, to his saving grace, was Reagan's engaging likability.

Likability Trumps Illegality?

Most Americans, much of official Washington, and many in the press corps simply liked Ronald Reagan too well to probe further into the abyss of Iran-Contra and risk finding something that would prove him to be personally culpable.

So maybe that is another lesson, Mr. President. If you are going to shred the Constitution, be a nice guy and you might get away with it. Also, make sure you have a spouse who knows when it's time to swing the ax and save your skin.

Coming as it did on the heels of decades of presidential usurpa-tion of war powers, the Iran-Contra scandal probably should have resulted in some sort of congressional censure of the president. Running a war without authority or funding was such a phenom-enal abuse of power that it might have been wise to put something on the record to guard against future presidents' trying anything of the kind.

But Congress has been woefully complaisant in the face of the expansion of presidential war powers, and thus has participated in the demise of its constitutionally given powers.

Good Choices Can Be Bad Politics

The loopholes that your predecessors have opened, Mr. President, will tempt you to make use of the expansive powers now available to the commander in chief. Few have resisted. The ability to order an air strike anywhere in the world is very seductive.

The problem is that you'll have no idea what you might unleash. The harder work of tough diplomacy will usually pay better long-term dividends for the country, even if it does not boost your approval ratings.

Jimmy Carter is an example of one recent president who resisted pressures to use the military option in several cases. Unfortunately for him, that resistance contributed to his unpopularity and failed reelection bid.

To the consternation of the intelligence community, Carter scaled back covert operations in places such as Iran and Nicaragua. For decades, the Central Intelligence Agency had propped up dictatorial regimes in both countries, producing a generation of citizens who hated us and dedicated their lives to killing Americans.

Carter's determination to honor human rights extended to his revulsion at using U.S. military and intelligence resources to support offending nations even if they were friendly to U.S. interests.

In the wake of Carter's drive to end our pattern of turning a blind eye toward friendly nations that violated basic human rights, the American-backed regimes in Iran and Nicaragua collapsed. In both cases, unfriendly leaders stepped in. Carter had naïvely hoped to gain honorable allies among those who replaced the bad guys.

But those difficulties still do not negate the rightness of Carter's decisions. His admirable focus on human rights was long overdue. The cause of the resulting chaos lies in the decades of wrong choices by earlier presidents in nurturing dictators. By the time Carter set things right, the ill will was too great to overcome, fostered by American support for leaders who used torture and other violations of basic rights to stay in power.

In Iran, those who hated America took hostages at our embassy in Tehran. The long-running crisis contributed to Carter's failed reelection bid in 1980. Still, Carter resisted pressure for a massive military intervention, approving only a limited exercise to try to rescue the hostages. But the mission was aborted before the would-be saviors ever got to Tehran, as two of the eight helicopters carrying them developed mechanical problems in the desert en route, and one helicopter crashed into a C-130 transport plane, killing eight crew members.

Carter's secretary of state, Cyrus Vance, had warned against the rescue mission. He had no faith in the workability of the plan to helicopter in, get the hostages, and fly out. But other advisers prevailed, and Carter green-lighted the mission.

After the mission failed, it became clear how poorly it had been planned. Weather conditions and other basic factors were not properly evaluated. The incident became a horrible embarrassment to the nation, a belittling episode on top of what had already become a humiliating experience.

To his credit, Carter took full responsibility for the rescue debacle—and an angry nation was only too happy to oblige by heaping on the blame.

Carter probably would have been politically better off ordering a bloody invasion of some sort. His preference for negotiation over conflict made him seem weak to many voters, something Reagan exploited in his successful campaign against Carter.

Carter made mistakes in handling the Iranian hostage crisis. And there are lessons for future presidents on what they should not do, but he made the right choice in avoiding a military escalation that would have cost many lives. Some might say Carter should have gone macho and rained a hail of bombs on Iran. But widening the conflict to a war would have made it all worse. Ironically, it was the military option he did choose that did him in.

Carter's political demise does not mean that his choices were not good for the country or the Constitution. The point is that sometimes the right decision is bad for your political standing, Mr. President. But again, in your inaugural oath, you did not swear to protect yourself.

Sometimes It's Best to Stay Behind the Scenes

Carter's biggest mistake was in so publicly getting involved in the negotiations to release the hostages. Privately directing his negotiators, while publicly going about other business, would have served him better. The presidential obsession fostered relentless media attention. Broadcaster Ted Koppel founded ABC's *Nightline* as a daily countdown of the hostage crisis, focusing on every nuance of every angle to the story.

Contrast that with a hostage-taking during the Vietnam era. While Johnson was in office, the North Vietnamese seized an American intelligence ship. It was a story on the day they were taken, and months later, when they were released, it was another story—with very little media focus in between.

Coming as it did in the year of his reelection campaign, the Iranian hostage crisis became the touchstone of Carter's entire administration. The election became a referendum on his failure to get the hostages released while in office.

History is treating him better. Carter's devotion to human rights was also his trademark as an ex-president, and won him the Nobel Prize years after he left office. His refusal to exploit the war powers available to him kept the hostage crisis from becoming a regional meltdown. Many lives were saved by a peace-loving president who put his ideals above his politics.

You would think that if Americans learned anything in the debacle that the Iraq War turned out to be, it would be that the nation's founders were absolutely correct in giving Congress the sole power to declare war. Only in this way can the people play a direct role in deciding whether it is necessary to send their children to their possible deaths abroad.

"Where Is Everybody?"

No war should ever be undertaken without a full and fair debate that engages all sides of the question, and Congress is the best forum for doing that. There was no debate on the question of authorizing George W. Bush to invade Iraq.

When the Senate finally scheduled what was supposed to be a debate, few lawmakers showed up. Senator Robert Byrd (D-W.Va.), a fierce advocate for restricting presidential war powers, looked around the nearly empty chamber that day and muttered to an aide, "Where is everybody?"

Byrd's question could be asked of the whole country. A president was planning to invade a country that had not provoked us. There was talk of a new doctrine of preemptive war, meaning that our policy from here on would be to invade those who might pose a threat, even if nothing specific had been done.

Where was everybody? Lawmakers on Capitol Hill detected little opposition or interest in the mail and phone calls they obsessively monitor from constituents. Reporters, bullied by the president's high approval ratings, asked few questions.

Surely the lesson of that time should be that presidents cannot be allowed to railroad the country into a war. If a democracy means anything, it is the right of the people to have their Congress assert its power to fully debate and clearly vote up or down any declaration of war. Yet the lesson, while learned by many, is no longer embedded in action or in law. The words are still in the Constitution, but they mean little after decades of congressional passiveness.

Despite rebukes, scandal, and plummeting popularity, presidents tend to exploit every opportunity to claim the right to almost unilaterally start a war. The new rule seems to be that presidents declare war and Congress gives permission. Even after ceding its supposedly exclusive power to declare war to the executive branch in the run-up to the Iraq invasion—and even after Democrats won control of Congress in 2006—the legislative branch failed again as the Bush administration signaled many times its intentions to step up hostilities against Iran.

Congress punted when faced with the direct question: Does the president of the United States have any authority for direct or covert (or privately contracted) action against Iran without congressional approval?

It is a question that official Washington avoids because the answer is that both major parties want to preserve the option to conduct war without congressional approval.

No matter which political party wins the presidency, the power to make war slips further toward the White House.

Citizens Should Beware a Powerful President

As important as preserving Congress's power to declare war ought to be for most Americans, there is another consequence of presidential overreaching that is equally dangerous to our rights. Our individual freedoms can be lost to a president's zeal in a time of war, especially as we face the threat of terrorists in our midst instead of standing armies abroad.

Periodically, these moments of testing have come for our nation—times of great fear and panic that stretch the limits of our faith in government to prevail without granting almost dictatorial powers to the president. And yet it is the act of ceding these extraordinary powers to the chief executive, not the events that led to it, that most threatens our ability to continue governing ourselves under the Constitution.

At the beginning of the twenty-first century we were tested again. The story of our response, sadly, became yet another cautionary tale for letting a president go too far when we are afraid.

There is no question that September 11, 2001, brought about many dramatic changes in our country, but perhaps the most long-lasting and frightening impact of that day's shocking attacks on U.S. soil was how fear of terrorism trumped America's faith in the right to liberty and individual privacy. Sadly, we had a president at the time who exploited every opportunity to convert public panic into a broad array of new powers for himself.

The great journalist Edward R. Murrow once said, "No one can terrorize a whole nation, unless we are all his accomplices." After 9/11 too many Americans became accomplices in their own loss of freedoms. Even just looking the other way makes one complicit.

Mr. President, before you are tempted to follow George W. Bush's example of power grabbing in a crisis, do not forget that ultimately he lost the public's support. Most Americans came to regret how willingly they let Bush assume powers beyond a president's normal reach.

For alleged security, we were willing to forgo our privacy and our great sense of justice. We permitted ourselves to be wiretapped, our e-mails pried into, our mail opened. We tolerated the torture of suspects and prisoners at Abu Ghraib and at prisons in Iraq and Guantánamo Bay, where human beings were humiliated.

Surely that was not worthy of a great country. We detained and imprisoned people with dark skin. We never charged them or gave them trials. We kept them in limbo and sent them to secret prisons to be tortured and interrogated. Was that America?

One day Americans will look back upon this era as we now look back at the outrageous detainment of Japanese-Americans during World War II, a practice also sanctioned by the Supreme Court. And yet we continued to witness even more violations of civil rights against more groups and individuals.

A culture of permissiveness toward governmental intervention in our lives can easily take hold in time of crisis—all in the name of national security. Pushing back at these times requires faith in our constitutional system of government and fierce resistance against attempts to move it aside until calmer days.

Panic Can Be Freedom's Loss

It was the Justice Department of the 1920s that conducted the so-called Palmer Raids, named for Woodrow Wilson's attorney general, Alexander Mitchell Palmer. In response to a series of bombings around the country during World War I, Palmer's agents seized thousands of books, records, and other writings from suspect groups, focusing on any with members who had foreign backgrounds. They conducted mass arrests, sometimes based solely on the national heritage of the suspects. President Wilson himself set the tone for these outrageous violations of individual rights, saying, "Hyphenated Americans . . . have poured the poison of disloyalty into the very arteries of our national life. Such creatures of passion, disloyalty and anarchy must be crushed out."

Many cases of the government's unlawful detentions and illegal entrapment were documented. And the courts were kept busy overturning bogus convictions.

Fast forward to our response to 9/11, and almost a century later we veered onto a similar path. It has been difficult for the news media to document much of what our government did in the name of rooting out enemies. In fact, to keep the news media from getting too feisty, the Justice Department sent a memo to federal agencies promising to back them up anytime they wanted to deny freedom of information requests from scholars and journalists. Protecting the government from criticism over the administration's clamp-down on rights was central to keeping the public at bay. People cannot complain about abuses they don't know about.

The news media bear much of the responsibility for keeping power-grabbing presidents in check. But too often reporters roll over and play dead when a president is on a roll. They become afraid of being called unpatriotic and un-American when the public is clamoring for a president to bend the rules. When journalists lose their gumption and do a lousy job of blowing the whistle, our rights suffer.

We cannot rely on well-intentioned presidents to care for our rights when they are protecting themselves or are driven by misguided notions about how to protect the nation's security. Fortunately, such presidents don't come around that often. Yet the pressures are great and opportunities abound for a president to bend or break the law to his will. And of all the ways in which a president can go beyond his constitutional powers, the most frightening and ominous are the assaults on human rights in times of war.

It is time to return to the true ideals of the Bill of Rights. The issue is not the right to live, but what kind of life. The issue is freedom without government or outside interference.

The country's tolerance of governmental abuses in times of emergency is like the proverbial camel's nose under the tent. The rights of the individual are being hacked away on all fronts.

Protecting Privacy

The debate over whether or how much the Constitution and the Bill of Rights protect an individual's privacy threatens to end up giving a wide berth for power-hungry politicians, especially to presidents.

The Supreme Court's first ruling that a privacy right exists was not that long ago. The significance of the 1973 *Roe v. Wade* decision was not that it wiped out state and federal laws that ban abortions. The significance was that the decision was based upon the much broader notion that the Constitution protects an individual's right to privacy.

Predictably and unfortunately, the Court's assault on *Roe* is narrowly seen as only about the right to abortion. The abortion debate, while important, should not overshadow how attacks against *Roe* are also attacks against a privacy right for everyone.

As the roster of justices changed in the decades after 1973, the *Roe* ruling has been repeatedly undermined by later decisions. The right to privacy has lost ground in the Supreme Court's drive to erase it from our jurisprudence.

This new age of downplaying individual rights for the "greater good" seems eerily similar to famous police states in history, such as those once run by communists or fascists. The result is a surveillance society that tolerates untold infringements by government and private industry.

But it is never too late to change, Mr. President. You can be the nation's chief protector of our rights, despite the pressures on you to go in the other direction. With appointments to the courts, the conduct of your Justice Department, and the tone of your words, you can send a message throughout the bureaucracy that, like yourself, the employees of the government work for the people, not against them.

Or, like Wilson in the 1920s, you can send a message that unleashes the beast against our own citizens, risking that the innocent, along with the guilty, are "crushed out."

The great strength of America is that we have stepped back from the breach whenever our own fears allowed presidents to go too far. We have overcome similar periods in past wars, including the infamous raids against private citizens during World War I, the wholesale detainment of Japanese-Americans during World War II, and the anticommunist hysteria of the Cold War.

Presidents should lead a backlash against the abuse of rights, not be the cause of the abuses. For that, we need presidents who truly value the constitutional limits on their powers and continually educate the citizenry about those limits.

They might start by now and then reminding us of their sole job description, to "preserve, protect and defend" the Constitution.

THREE

WATCH YOUR IMAGE:
YOU'RE ON YOUTUBE

A desire to be observed, considered, esteemed, praised, beloved, and admired by his fellows is one of the earliest as well as the keenest dispositions discovered in the heart of man.

—JOHN ADAMS

Take care with the image that you present to the country and to the rest of the world, Mr. President. For maintaining confidence in your leadership, how you look and sound in the media age can sometimes matter more than the decisions you make.

Acting presidential is not always the same as appearing presidential.

In the modern media age, we look at presidents nearly every day, and how we react to their appearance can affect what we think of them. The advent of viral video on the Internet, such as YouTube, makes it possible for anyone in the world to see every frame of a president's every move in public.

But even before the modern age, appearances mattered.

Abraham Lincoln was actually the first to exploit the use of photography to enhance his image. While he was one of our greatest presidents, his gaunt face and gangly frame certainly kept him out of the ranks of our best-looking chief executives.

Photographer Mathew Brady took great care to improve how Lincoln looked in a widely reproduced campaign photo. Brady pulled up Lincoln's collar to cover his long neck and retouched his face. Lincoln also grew a beard in response to advice that it would hide his less-than-attractive face.

But a fitting image is not just about physicality, Mr. President. The factors in crafting a popular presentation range from being politically correct in your language to avoiding embarrassment on a personal or political scale.

Otherwise competent presidents gained negative reputations from the smallest things.

Poor Gerald Ford was caught on videotape falling down the rain-soaked steps to Air Force One during a state visit to Austria, and never lived it down. Despite being one of the better athletes in presidential history, Ford earned a reputation for being clumsy, fueling the career of comic Chevy Chase for his falling-down impersonations.

Other odd presidential moments did not become overriding impressions, as in Ford's case, but certainly didn't help.

Bill Clinton, known for sleeping as little as four hours a night, was occasionally caught nodding off during public events. His fluctuating weight—and love for fast food—was a popular topic around the watercooler.

George W. Bush became the joke sensation of late-night talk shows when he hastily tried to exit a Beijing news conference and ran smack into a locked door.

But for unparalleled embarrassment it is hard to top Bush's father, George H. W. Bush, who was filmed at a state dinner in Japan vomiting on the host country's prime minister.

Taft's Tub Flub

Presidents who served before the media age were lucky. Imagine the unkind fat jokes that would target our weightiest president, William Howard Taft. At over three hundred thirty pounds, Taft's girth was quite the laughing matter, even without the technology for constant visual reminders of it.

Taft once sent a telegram to a cabinet member, saying, "Went on a horse ride today; feeling good." The recipient replied, "How's the horse?"

When Taft could not dislodge himself from the White House bathtub, it took four construction workers to remove him and required the procurement of an oversized bathtub that was seven feet long and three and a half feet wide. News accounts of the removal of the old tub reported that it was cracked, prompting widespread belief that Taft had actually broken his tub. White House officials insisted that it was damaged during the removal.

History can be so unfair. Although an accomplished president, Taft is best remembered for getting stuck in the tub.

Beware how the silliest of incidents or a single unflattering photograph can undermine your image, Mr. President. Nothing is off the record. If you want a private life, don't become president. That was how some of us in the press corps saw it when aides to Bill and Hillary Clinton threw a fit over a news media photograph of the two of them vacationing at the beach.

Barack Obama similarly showed displeasure early in the 2008 presidential campaign when a picture of him in his bathing suit made the rounds in celebrity magazines. It happened again when he went on vacation in Hawaii after the election. Luckily for Obama, his trim physique did not provoke the ridicule that the less-fit Clintons experienced in their supposedly unguarded moment.

Sorry, Mr. President, but when you take up residence in the White House, you had better understand that you live in a fishbowl with few hiding places. You are public property. Don't go into public life if you want a private life.

Presidents are so shielded from the normal routines of life that they might be forgiven for thinking they are somehow protected from everything. The psychological impact of isolation, despite constant scrutiny, is one for the medical experts to figure out. But it is often humorous to watch them wrestle with their surreal circumstances.

Sometimes they never see it coming. Seemingly insignificant events in their daily lives can quickly become national sensations. The more weird they are, the more attention they get. And the more attention they get, the more they threaten to become a president's overshadowing image.

"Quiet! I've Been Shot."

Sometimes an unplanned moment works well to underscore a positive image. Theodore Roosevelt nurtured a cult of personality based upon an image of invincibility and can-do spirit that came to represent a growing and ambitious nation.

Although occurring after his presidency, Roosevelt's amazing survival of an assassination attempt could serve as a metaphor for the mystical ideal of the modern presidency's larger-than-life reach. While Roosevelt was giving a speech in Wisconsin, a saloon-keeper shot him in the chest with a revolver. To the astonishment of the crowd, Roosevelt kept giving his speech, only referring to the incident by saying, "Quiet! I've been shot."

What his audience didn't know was that a one-hundred-page speech folded over twice and a metal glasses case in Roosevelt's breast pocket had slowed the bullet. He later went to the hospital, but refused to have the bullet removed, remembering that President William McKinley had died after operations to remove an assassin's bullet.

Imagine the awe of that crowd watching a great leader unfazed by a speeding bullet lodged in his chest.

Unfortunately, for some, unexpected moments overtake them in less positive ways and instead reinforce a negative image.

One Crazed Rabbit

Jimmy Carter tangled with a crazed rabbit on a fishing trip near his Georgia home and it became a headline grabber for days, prompting his former press secretary, Jody Powell, to try to set the record straight in a book about his White House years, *The Other Side of the Story.*

Powell's account of how the story began and then mushroomed out of control provides a textbook example for how a president's private life can become distracting front-page news when he least expects it:

It began late one afternoon in the spring of 1979. The President was sitting with a few of us on the Truman Balcony. He had recently returned from a visit to Plains, and we were talking about homefolks and how the quail were nesting and similar matters of international import.

Suddenly, for no apparent reason—he was drinking lemonade, as I recall—the President volunteered the information that while fishing in a pond on his farm he had sighted a large animal swimming toward him. Upon closer inspection, the animal turned out to be a rabbit. Not one of your cutesy, Easter Bunny–type rabbits, but one of those big splay-footed things that we called swamp rabbits when I was growing up.

The animal was clearly in distress, or perhaps berserk. The President confessed to having had limited experience with enraged rabbits. He was unable to reach a definite conclusion about its state of mind. What was obvious, however, was that this large, wet animal, making strange hissing noises and gnashing its teeth, was intent upon climbing into the Presidential boat.

Apparently, the president shooed the offending rabbit away with his paddle. The story would have died of natural causes had Powell not made the mistake of passing it along to a reporter, Brooks Jackson of CNN. Still, the reporter wrote the story in a lighthearted fashion. Powell wrongly thought it would be received as a "mildly amusing incident" and laughed it off.

"We were soon corrected," Powell writes in his book.

The *Washington Post*, exercising the news judgment that we in the White House had come to appreciate so keenly, headed the piece "President Attacked by Rabbit" and ran it on the front page. The more cautious *New York Times* boxed it on page A-12. That night, all three networks found time to report the amazing incident. But that was just the beginning.

It was a nightmare. The story ran for more than a week. The President was repeatedly asked to explain his behavior at town hall meetings, press conferences, and meetings with editors.

There was talk of a suit under the Freedom of Information Act to force release of the picture showing the President, paddle and rabbit in close proximity.

Shortly after the Reagan administration took office, they stumbled upon a copy of the picture—apparently while searching for a foreign policy—and reopened the old wounds by releasing it to the press.

It just goes to show that the most innocent or mundane moments, when experienced by a president, can cause quite a ruckus.

Poor Harry Truman decided to walk on his own to the bank across the street from the White House one day and caused a public spectacle as a crowd thronged around him without any security. Frantic Secret Service agents scrambled to the scene and pulled him away.

Determined to lead a normal life at the White House, Truman still insisted on strolling outside the White House to walk his dog, buy newspapers, and continue depositing his paycheck at the bank. Unable to persuade the president to give up this potentially dangerous practice, they tried to accommodate him by rigging traffic lights to turn red in all four directions.

Keep Your Image Down to Earth

Truman's famous walkabouts, while probably not calculated to do so, enhanced his image as a man of the people.

It is important to find genuine ways to show yourself down to earth, Mr. President.

Living in their protective bubble as they do, presidents can be forgiven for losing touch with how normal people live. But often their zeal for personal privacy contributes to their own isolation. Soon, their public appearances tend to become tightly scripted and the visuals managed, right down to dictating the camera angles that photographers are allowed to use.

Understandably, modern presidential staffs are obsessed with the dangers of an embarrassing gaffe or unappealing photo. But it does not well serve a president to limit his appearances to one-dimensional images.

Presidents are conflicted by the lines between their public and private lives. Like Hollywood celebrities, they want the attention, but on their own terms. Fame, however, usually comes on the public's terms, not those of the famous.

In a presidential campaign, candidates necessarily keep the focus on themselves. They are, after all, the ones we are voting for. Those who must struggle for attention seek any opportunity for the limelight. Once elected, however, many presidents spend more time seeking the shadows as the limelight they once craved begins to scorch. It never fails.

Having a cup of coffee with a presidential candidate in Iowa at the start of a campaign is about as easy as chatting with a shoe salesman. But as they start winning, the clamp-down begins. More aides than ever surround them. Fewer press conferences are scheduled and access is doled out like precious stones. By the time they get to the White House, the battle to control image and information reaches a fever pitch and never lets up.

Johnson's "Strange Bedroom" Warning

Image is so important to presidents. They hire an army of consultants, pollsters, and ad makers to turn them into something more than human. Anything that might tarnish that image is subject to a cover-up.

Lyndon Johnson once privately gathered some of the men in the White House press corps to issue what some thought to be a rather presumptuous demand. He told them that he didn't expect them to count how many drinks he took or when he went into a "strange bedroom."

Naturally, quite a discussion ensued among reporters after that exchange. Was the president giving them orders? Interestingly, some of the men thought so, while some of the women in the press corps, upon hearing about it, felt the president was just teasing, or bluffing. Johnson was prone to swagger at times and make outrageous statements in these off-the-record moments with the news media.

Johnson knew better than to assume that he could order the press around. Still, he basically was saying that he didn't expect to be watched that closely when he was off the reservation. And in those days that more or less was the rule. We now know much more about Kennedy's escapades than we did at the time. While many in the press corps gossiped about his womanizing, it was not publicly reported.

Fast forward to the Clinton years and you can see how Kennedy's image could have been vastly different. Indeed, in Kennedy's more conservative time, confirmed reports of ongoing presidential adultery could have derailed his presidency far more than it did for Clinton.

Some in the news media, who knew the most about Kennedy's extracurricular activities, had become personal friends with him and protected him. That is always a danger to maintaining a professional distance. Kennedy had been in Washington a long time, served in the House and Senate. He had made a lot of friends in the press corps, had been a newspaper man himself at one point.

Basically, Kennedy charmed the press corps into looking the other way. It is best for reporters not to take off their press hat when socializing with politicians.

Journalists Should Not Be Image Makers

Far too often in modern times journalists become enablers of a president's manufactured image. That is why it is so important for reporters to keep their distance and always be "on the clock" anytime they are with the president.

Those of us who insisted on wearing our press badges when covering White House social evenings, for instance, sometimes irritated press secretaries who thought it was tacky. But however it is done, by wearing a badge or making it clear in conversation, reporters should never try to hide the fact that they are the news media. Although there were lapses, as in Kennedy's time, presidents should not assume that a reporter is their friend. And no reporter should make the compromising mistake of trying to be the personal friend of a president.

Perhaps the Kennedy case was an example of giving the president too much personal space. But the media rule in Washington at the time was that a politician's personal life was off the record unless it affected his public work. Up to that point, the reporters just gossiped to each other.

These days, of course, gossip gets reported. There are no rules anymore. Clinton obviously thought the old Kennedy rules would apply or he would not have risked the affair with Monica Lewinsky. How dumb. Right or wrong, the new rule is that everything is fair game.

Abandoning protective coverage rules seems to have come along as presidents and their staffs became more sophisticated at crafting images that sometimes were far from the truth. Presidents are different from most anyone in public life. We expect them to live like preachers. Hollywood stars can behave like wild animals and we get a kick out their escapades. It even makes us more likely to go see their movies. Athletes are no longer held to the high standards of personal behavior that they once were. But we think a president is supposed to be better than the rest of us. They are not. They live with just as many demons as the average person, maybe more. It would be nice if we just recognized that and let them be.

When they act holier than thou, however, maybe the new rules are justified. Let it all be told.

"About the Same Percentage of Criminals Here as in the Rest of the Population"

Presidents might be less obsessed with creating illusions about themselves if the voters were more realistic. It is a mistake to expect politicians to be pure. The nature of the business calls forth those who are morally relative. The game of politics attracts manipulators, Type A personalities, and would-be Machiavellians.

Former Speaker of the House Jim Wright once told the blunt truth when pressed to defend members of Congress who were being accused of committing crimes. He responded by noting that the House was a truly representative body. "We've got about the same percentage of criminals here as in the rest of the population," he said.

The best advice for voters seeking moral leadership would be to go see your preacher. Looking to politicians for it will probably leave you disappointed.

For young people interested in a political life, for your sake hopefully you will decide to do so at the age of five and live accordingly, because your life, your family, your finances, everything will be open sesame.

There is no safety from public view, Mr. President. Right or wrong, even your bedroom is on the record—especially if, as in Clinton's case, the Oval Office becomes an extension of your bedroom.

Still, Clinton survived a Senate impeachment trial for lying about his adulterous affairs, perhaps proving that presidents need not worry too much about embarrassing facts of their personal lives getting out.

A "Lovable Rogue"

Clinton's image with the public was complex. Even his naughty side seemed to contribute to a sense that at least we knew the real person. An Arkansas friend of Clinton's once dubbed this phenomenon the "lovable rogue" syndrome.

Most people really liked Clinton, and because his lusty side had been explored during his first presidential campaign, in the long run the public was probably not too surprised that it continued during his presidency. By the end of Clinton's second term, the news media and his political foes had lower ratings in the opinion polls.

The courage and stamina that Clinton showed as his dirty laundry became a national obsession was truly remarkable, and in a very odd way gave many Americans confidence in his leadership.

Around reporters, Clinton remained amazingly calm during those difficult times, never saying a mean thing about those who were torturing him, even though so many of the politicians who attacked him led personal lives that were hardly above reproach. The bottom line is that he never should have been subjected to the kind of tyranny against his personal life that the press and political opponents aimed at him.

Although Clinton was able to compartmentalize his personal trials and continue to get things done, his presidency probably achieved less than it could have because of the ongoing distractions. He was under fire so much of the time.

Presidential Vacations

How they spend their vacations can even become a factor in presidential image making.

Early in his first term, Bill Clinton, who did not own a personal retreat, gave a lot of thought to the political ramifications of how best to vacation. Pundits in Washington argued about where the president should go as if it was a weighty matter of policy.

One year, the Clintons chose elite Martha's Vineyard in Massachusetts, setting off a torrent of criticism that the president was too cozy with the many celebrities who live there or spend their summers on the tony island. Noting that the Kennedy family retreat was in nearby Hyannis Port, critics accused Clinton of trying to be one of them.

John Kennedy embraced his own wealth by vacationing at his family's plush retreat in Palm Beach, Florida. In his case, the posh image underscored a popular desire to see him and his photogenic family as American royalty.

Images of the Kennedys in seaside bliss never seemed to rankle the naysayers. Instead, the nation was fixated on those pictures, almost as if getting some assurance that in a troubled world beset by the nuclear age, having a president who was able to relax meant that the rest of us could as well.

In recent years, it has become traditional for these presidential retreats to take on the airs of the White House itself, transferring its image of authority and power to vacation homes.

Aides re-create makeshift versions of their White House work spaces. A press room is established. Official signs are made saying things like the "Western White House," as was done in the cases of George W. Bush, Ronald Reagan, Richard Nixon, and Lyndon Johnson.

George H. W. Bush's seaside mansion in Maine, along with the expensive speedboat he kept there, delivered the opposite effect from what Kennedy experienced. In his case, it served up the image of a patrician lifestyle that didn't sit well with the American people as a recession hit the economy during the president's last couple of years in office.

Bush's son was well aware that a Kennebunkport-style retreat was a bit over the top. Instead, George W. Bush bought a Texas ranch with plenty of land to buffer away the onlookers—and the press in particular.

The president and his staff were almost paranoid about deflecting unwanted attention at the ranch in Crawford, Texas. A White House reporter on a road trip to Dallas innocently asked a local party official for directions to Crawford; later that day the president's press secretary called, suspiciously asking, "Why are you going to the ranch?" He was told that it was a just a field trip to the town to see what it was like.

Camp Sheehan

Ultimately, the Bush ranch did not forge the image of a down-to-earth president that he had hoped. Instead, it became the symbol of a burgeoning peace movement protesting the war in Iraq.

It was near the ranch in the summer of 2005 that Cindy Sheehan, the mother of an American soldier killed in Iraq, staged a month-long protest that became a focal point for an increasing number of citizens who had grown tired of the war.

On some days as many as fifteen hundred supporters visited "Camp Casey," named for Sheehan's deceased son, including members of Congress, as well as several notable actors, singers, and civil rights activists.

In a moment that seemed to underscore how Bush was out of touch with the public mood, his motorcade of limousines and police escorts indifferently sped by the makeshift camp of antiwar activists.

That image of indifference to dissent haunted his presidency from then on.

"I Feel Like I'm Dressing the Washington Monument"

First Ladies and their children are major factors in presidential image. They endure endless speculation, criticism, and fascination with seemingly mundane matters.

After a particularly intense round of fashion controversy about Eleanor Roosevelt's somewhat frumpy look, she famously said, "Sometimes I feel like I'm dressing the Washington Monument."

Eleanor also once said, "Sure, you can have a personal life—if you don't do anything and just sit in the White House."

Imagine what a "colorful" First Lady such as Mary Todd Lincoln would experience in today's media environment. Even in those discreet times, Washington gossips stayed quite busy telling stories about her emotional outbursts. Lincoln himself had to intervene with Congress when his wife's profligate spending at the White House outraged lawmakers.

It later turned out that Mrs. Lincoln was mentally ill and deserved the compassion that her patient husband showed to her. Such a spouse in the White House these days would probably get little sympathy, only the crushing attention of the public's appetite for juicy stories.

Being First Lady is not such a bad thing, of course. Many enter the White House hoping to stay behind the scenes, but come to enjoy the unique opportunities to make a difference and contribute to maintaining a positive image for their husbands.

Hubert Humphrey's wife, Muriel, was once asked why she would want to be First Lady. "Because I can wave a magic wand," she said.

Another potential First Lady, Tipper Gore, displayed a different view when interviewed as her husband, Al, accepted the Democratic presidential nomination in the summer of 2000. When asked how she would serve, a seemingly irritated Tipper said, "I have a life of my own."

"I'm Just Going to Take Care of Ronnie"

Nancy Reagan, who became a force in focusing the nation's attention on drug abuse, had no such ambitions at the start of her husband's presidency. Asked what her project would be, Mrs. Reagan said, "I'm just going to take care of Ronnie."

If only it were that simple. As Mrs. Reagan soon learned, a First Lady is expected to take on semi-official duties even though it is not really an official government post—and with no salary, of course.

Juggling official and family duties can be especially tough for a presidential spouse with young children.

Hillary Rodham Clinton was remarkably successful in maintaining a somewhat normal life for her daughter, Chelsea, despite the peering eyes of the modern age. The Clintons implored the news media to leave Chelsea alone. Mostly, it worked.

At age thirteen when the Clintons entered the White House, Chelsea spent her teen years largely out of the public eye. It helped that she was a good kid who seemed to take her odd life in stride, showing no signs of abusing the privileges of a White House existence. It probably helped the president overcome his adultery problem that so many Americans respected the job that he and Hillary had done as parents. Even their most vocal critics often gave them credit for that much.

Chelsea's positive experience with the media in the White House was not shared by other teenagers living there. Gerald and Betty

Ford's four children, ranging in age from seventeen to twenty-four, stirred up a bevy of stories about White House romps. Unfortunately for the Fords, they developed an image as the parents of spoiled brats.

Former NBC White House correspondent Tom Brokaw talked about the Ford children in a 2008 television interview when NBC late-night host Conan O'Brien asked him to identify the "wildest" children to live in the White House.

"Ford had these very handsome, very robust teenage boys," Brokaw replied. "I think more than a few dates of the Ford boys got to see the Lincoln Bedroom in ways that probably a lot of other people had not. And there might even have been some controlled substances that were used, in the interest of experimentation."

The Fords presented an usual case of a family unexpectedly thrust into a White House life with almost no preparation. Vice President Gerald Ford had never run for president and suddenly succeeded to office in 1974 when Richard Nixon resigned.

There was not even a vice presidential mansion in those days. The Ford family lived a normal suburban life in Virginia safely beyond public scrutiny until suddenly becoming the nation's First Family. With no experience in avoiding the press, the Ford children and their antics did get plenty of attention around office watercoolers throughout the country.

Younger children in the White House, naturally, are a bit easier to control, but generate just as much public fascination. Caroline and "John John" Kennedy were as famous as their parents during their father's time in office. Both were photogenic, playful, and, despite being so young, accustomed to the privileged and public life they led.

Jackie Kennedy was fiercely protective of her children's privacy, directing aides to rebuke reporters and photographers who violated her sense of what was appropriate. But even Jackie could be somewhat ambivalent about a perceived invasion. While she complained about press photos of her children, often the photographer would get a quiet request from her East Wing office for copies of the supposedly offending pictures. Many were later prominently displayed in the Kennedy presidential library.

Jackie Kennedy played the role of reluctant public figure as though she did not want any coverage. Of course, that made the news media all the more rabid.

There is a lesson in her ways for politicians who might really want more coverage. Acting as though you do not want it serves to whet the press corps' appetite.

The Kennedy family was especially fascinating because the parents and the children were so much younger than any who had lived in the White House before. Following eight years of a much older couple, the Eisenhowers, the young Kennedy family embodied the popular image of a new generation taking charge of the country. Indeed, a "new generation" was JFK's campaign slogan in 1960.

Reporters could not resist writing about the Kennedy children. It was exciting and amusing to watch these little kids in the museum of the White House, saying and doing cute things. The press played its own hide-and-seek game with Jackie and her children. Of course, her husband's advisers knew quite well that the coverage was politically advantageous for their White House—one reason they, too, often wanted extra copies of the photographs.

Barack and Michelle Obama's family also underscore an image of change that was central to his election. It was the first time since the Kennedy years that such young children accompanied such young parents.

The public enjoys watching Obama's two daughters. Their parents share some of Jackie's ambivalence about protecting their privacy. They also seem to enjoy the attention that she privately relished.

"I Think That We Got Carried Away in the Moment"

Indeed, the Obamas are more prone to feature their children than the Clintons had been with Chelsea. So much so that they stirred a bit of controversy in the summer of the 2008 campaign by sitting down for a four-part television interview of the entire family on a tabloid-style entertainment program.

At the time of the interview on NBC's *Access Hollywood,* Obama's daughter Malia was ten years old and Sasha was seven. The engaging and talkative girls got as much airtime as their parents. Later, questions arose about whether Obama was using his daughters for political gain; the presidential candidate responded that he should have been more protective.

"I think that we got carried away in the moment," said Obama, who by this time was the presumed Democratic nominee. "We were having a birthday party, and everybody was laughing. And suddenly this thing cropped up. I didn't catch it quickly enough. I was surprised by the attention it received."

Cute kids in the White House—like the rest of your personal life—are simply irresistible for the press and the public, Mr. President. Just be careful about finding that balance between protecting their privacy and indulging the public's interest. Once the door is opened to making your children fair game, stories can emerge that do not enhance your image as you might hope.

Obama wrestles with another issue that he certainly does not want to be part of his image: his smoking. Gerald Ford was the last president before him to use tobacco products. He smoked a pipe, about eight bowls a day, and wasn't shy about it. Ford even posed for an official portrait holding a pipe. But in the years since Ford the country turned virulently against smoking. The White House was declared a smoke-free zone. That rule was imposed by Hillary Rodham Clinton when she was First Lady. Since Obama made Clinton his secretary of state, perhaps she will give him a break.

Obama reportedly began smoking cigarettes about two decades before his election. He vowed to quit at the start of his campaign. Trying to quit cigarettes while undergoing the stress of running for president was apparently difficult for him.

In an interview with NBC's Tom Brokaw after the election, Obama was evasive about the status of his smoking habit.

"Have you stopped smoking?" Brokaw asked.

"I have," Obama replied, smiling broadly. "What I said was that there are times where I have fallen off the wagon."

"Wait a minute," Brokaw interjected, "that means you haven't stopped."

"Fair enough," Obama said. "What I would say is that I have

done a terrific job under the circumstances of making myself much healthier. You will not see any violations of these rules in the White House."

It is so difficult for presidents to admit any personal failings. They are expected to present a near perfect image as role models. But could it be too much pressure? The presidency is difficult enough without demanding perfection in their personal lives. But the desire to appear flawless drives presidents to conceal things that the public probably would forgive.

Americans are getting better than presidents might expect at focusing on the work they do and overlooking distasteful personal matters. The public was displeased with Clinton's womanizing but still gave him high approval ratings in the polls.

Even Nixon's notorious cursing, so well documented on his White House tapes, would not have been so shocking to the nation if he had not presented such a different image in public.

You are not perfect, Mr. President. So don't pretend that you are and hide the bad stuff. If you smoke and can't stop, say so.

Keeping a Healthy Image

Health-related matters are often highly sensitive for presidents. A serious medical problem can seriously undermine the image of robust leader. Naturally, presidents are not fond of the whole world poring over their medical records. Who would be?

But the country needs to know whether or not the commander in chief remains fit for office. At least two of our presidents, we later learned, ended their days in office virtually incapacitated.

Despite Wilson's vigorous golfing, he suffered a stroke in 1919 that was far more damaging than the public knew. The physical strain from his demanding public speaking tour to promote American membership in the League of Nations is thought to have caused the stroke. He collapsed in Pueblo, Colorado, after one of his final speeches on the nationwide tour.

Less than a month later Wilson suffered his most serious stroke, one that left him paralyzed on his left side and blind in his left eye. Confined to a wheelchair for months, he never regained the ability to walk without assistance. The extent of Wilson's complete incapacitation was kept hidden from the public throughout the final two years of his presidency and even until after his death in 1924.

His own vice president, his cabinet, and members of Congress were kept away in a dramatic effort to conceal the president's condition. Wilson's second wife, Edith Bolling Wilson, very nearly ran the country. She controlled his schedule, upstaged his chief of staff, decided which official papers he would read, and dispatched orders to his cabinet.

What the public also did not know is that Wilson had suffered a stroke before becoming president, at age thirty-nine. That first stroke cost him the central vision in his left eye. Severe hypertension in his adult years is believed to have put him at risk for the debilitating strokes.

Franklin Roosevelt's condition before he died in office is still something of a mystery. His medical records disappeared just two days after his death.

More than a year before Roosevelt died at his cottage in Warm Springs, Georgia, those around him began noticing a serious deterioration in his health. He was complaining of severe headaches at night. He lost weight and grew weak, sometimes even blacking out while at his desk. During this time Roosevelt would frequently nod off during conversations. Once he blacked out while signing his name to a letter, leaving a long scrawl.

Amazingly, FDR's miserable health was kept mostly hidden. Perhaps because he had been president for so long, no one could imagine that he was mortal.

Medical historians have long tried to learn just what was wrong with him, but the disappearance of his records has made it more like detective work. Roosevelt's own doctor appears to be the prime suspect. The president's medical records were kept in the safe at Bethesda Naval Hospital. Only three people had access to it: two hospital officers and their superior officer, Admiral Ross McIntire, FDR's personal doctor.

McIntire was on the hook for publicly insisting that Roosevelt's health was fine during the months before the president's death. If those records showed otherwise, he would have had plenty of explaining to do.

"He kept information from the public, not only during Roosevelt's lifetime but even after Roosevelt had died," said Harry Goldsmith, author of *A Conspiracy of Silence: The Health and Death of Franklin D. Roosevelt*. McIntire was "saying that Roosevelt was always in excellent health, and we know that this is not the case," Goldsmith said.

Roosevelt's political team had a powerful incentive to keep his condition quiet. He was running for a fourth term at the time that his health declined, and there were many rumors that he was not up to another term in office. One of his close friends, a surgeon, was so concerned that he wrote a memorandum predicting that Roosevelt would not survive a fourth term. But it was not made public, and did not surface until years later in a court challenge to release it.

These dramatic examples of covering up the condition of incapacitated presidents eventually compelled the country to change the Constitution and provide a process for transferring power, at least temporarily, when a president is disabled. But the Twenty-fifth Amendment was not enacted until 1967, more than two decades after Roosevelt's death and more than forty years after Wilson's.

By the time of the amendment's passage, the president in office—Lyndon Johnson—was perhaps a bit too forthcoming about medical matters. While recuperating from gallbladder surgery, he raised his shirt to show his scar to assembled reporters and photographers. The image of a president's surgery scar immediately circled the globe, prompting a letter writer to the *New York Times* to remark, "God forbid he should have a hemorrhoidectomy!"

You don't have to show us all your scars, Mr. President, but get used to it. Your medical history, your personal flaws, and just about anything else we can think of is going to be public property.

On second thought, let's see those scars.

FOUR
Open Up:
The People Have a Right to Know

We are not afraid to entrust the American people with unpleasant facts, foreign ideas, alien philosophies, and competitive values. For a nation that is afraid to let its people judge the truth and falsehood in an open market is a nation that is afraid of its people.
—John F. Kennedy

Mr. President, your office surely is a bully pulpit, as Theodore Roosevelt dubbed it, but you will also need a functioning relationship with the White House press corps to be successful.

Direct contact with the citizens, whether by televised address or town halls with "civilians," is vital for maintaining your connection with the public. But to encourage public confidence in your leadership you also need to prove to the country that you can handle being questioned by reporters who test the logic, truthfulness, and competence of your administration.

In other words, the bully pulpit is not just for preaching to the choir. You must also develop your skills in handling the dreaded press conference, and in managing a staff that, while protecting you from undue harm, gains a reputation with the press corps for candor and professionalism.

The Direct Approach

There are times when a direct address to the public, rather than a press conference, fosters a sense of openness and accessibility.

But there other times it is used as propaganda, or, worse, to tell lies.

Of course, there are moments of national urgency when a president has every right to explain a major policy initiative, rally the public to his side, or warn the nation of an impending threat without critical questions that distract from his message. (So long as the opportunity for those questions eventually comes.)

Franklin Roosevelt's famous fireside chats during the Great Depression inspired confidence that someone was in charge and making a difference during tough times. But FDR remained available to reporters on a regular basis.

As the only elected official who is on every ballot in the nation, the president enjoys a unique bond with all Americans, and direct conversations with the public help nurture that connection.

Many presidents might have avoided a worsening of their problems had they chosen an earlier opportunity to address the nation on a pressing topic. The later years of Ronald Reagan's presidency were dominated by the Iran-Contra scandal because he took so long to finally acknowledge what was done and take responsibility for it in a nationally televised address.

Bill Clinton might have avoided impeachment and a Senate trial if he had initially chosen to tell the truth in a direct statement to the people, instead of lying about his affair with a young intern.

Going Over Our Heads

Still, a near-even balance of direct appeals and press conferences is called for. You need to develop a flair for both skills, Mr. President.

Naturally, presidents enjoy their role as "campaigner in chief." They're good at it. That's how they got elected. As a result, they predictably come across much better in a public appearance with supporters than they do in a press conference where there are no applause lines.

In a two-day cycle early in Barack Obama's presidency we saw a striking contrast between his studied, somber, and somewhat defensive stance in a press conference, followed by a town hall with a friendly audience the next morning. He was much more effective, warm, and engaging in the town hall.

Obama deserves credit for trying to achieve some balance between how many press conferences he gives versus his direct appeals to the public. So while journalists like ourselves might occasionally gripe about "going over our heads" to deliver a one-sided, unchallenged speech, we get it. Those direct appeals work. Just as long as you submit to regular scrutiny that goes beyond your talking points.

It is when a president tips the balance toward only giving speeches without opportunities for questions that he risks a reputation for a lack of openness. As much as Americans, particularly the president's most ardent supporters, express irritation at the press nagging, they understand that in a democracy the nation's leader ought to be open to challenging questions.

How to Survive the Press Corps

The first rule of the dreaded press conference, Mr. President, is to answer the question. Even "No comment" can be an answer. It's certainly better than dodging tough questions with diversionary non-answers when the people have a right to know. And lying is even worse than dodging.

How your staff deals with the press is up to you, Mr. President. Your own attitudes toward the news media will trickle down. If you see us as the enemy to be thwarted at every turn, things will deteriorate. If you value the media's role as a conduit to the public for explaining your decisions and relaying your forthright defenses against criticism, things will go better.

Presidents usually come into office vowing to conduct the most open administration in history. In the White House press room, we tend to snicker at such promises.

The openness or secrecy of an administration depends on the president. It is your job, Mr. President, to set the tone and lay down the rules for how your White House staff views the public's right to the truth.

There are many avenues available to a president to get his message out—the news media, addresses to the nation, and going on the stump. You will regret using those methods to avoid tough questions, distort the truth, or try to spin away your problems. It might take a while, but the public will one day catch on.

Truth sometimes takes time to get out, but it eventually surfaces. To paraphrase Mark Twain, a lie can circle the globe many times while the truth is still putting on its pants.

A president's relationship with the news media is the first and most obvious stop in evaluating a new administration's attitude toward the public's right to know the truth. Signs of a secretive, potentially self-destructive presidency include avoidance of presidential press conferences, recriminations against critical reporting, and excessive efforts to turn the public against the news media.

A Hostile Beginning

While most presidents promise openness, others come into office with a hostile attitude toward the press. Bill Clinton had a chip on his shoulder from day one as a result of the probing coverage of his personal life and background in the 1992 campaign.

As with any president, Clinton's attitude toward the press trickled down the White House hierarchy. Unlike others—such as Gerald Ford, who began with positive relations because he had many friends in the Washington press corps from years of service on Capitol Hill—Clinton was suspicious and distant with most reporters.

Both Bill and Hillary Clinton felt that the news media had treated them unfairly in the campaign. They had gone through quite a siege, with revelations of his affairs and criticism of her aggressive role in the campaign. And their distrust of the news media carried over to their early days in the White House.

Even before the Clintons officially moved in there was a minor dustup with the news media over rumors that the new First Lady wanted to convert a portion of the press room into offices for some of her staff. Hillary was determined to gain some turf in the West Wing instead of having her people confined to the traditional East Wing digs for the First Lady's offices. The White House press corps's outrage at giving up any part of our already cramped offices headed off what could have been a nasty confrontation.

Presidents and their teams have long yearned to move the press out of the West Wing where all the action is. Most would prefer to have us in the adjacent Old Executive Office Building, where we can be kept away from top White House aides. But the press corps is fiercely protective of our West Wing turf; we see it as an important showcase for our democracy that the pesky media are right there at the presidential doorstep holding them accountable.

Even a few former White House press secretaries agree. In his book, *The Twilight of the Presidency*, George Reedy, who served under Lyndon Johnson, writes about the importance of keeping the press corps so close to the president.

"Of the few social institutions which tend to keep a president in touch with reality, the most effective—and the most resented by the chief beneficiary—is the press," Reedy wrote in 1970. "It is the only force to enter the White House from the outside world with a direct impact on the man in the Oval Room which cannot be softened by intermediary interpreters or deflected by sympathetic attendants."

Reedy notes that the benefit to presidents in having frequent encounters with reporters in his midst "does not arise out of any special integrity" they have, but comes from their basic purpose of keeping the public informed and the president in touch with reality. "No matter how sympathetically that function is performed, a foolish act will appear foolish, an unpopular act will arouse antagonism, and an act in conflict with previous actions will appear contradictory."

If presidents were dictators and unaccountable to the public, they could certainly do without having a gaggle of irritating truth seekers snapping at their feet. Reality could be whatever they wanted it to be. But Mr. President, you are accountable to the public and you will sorely regret not taking full advantage of your press corps as an early-warning system for problems in your administration that might eventually unsettle the voters.

Despite those benefits, a long line of presidents and their teams sought to erect barriers between themselves and White House correspondents.

It might not mean that we actually learn a lot more by being located inside the president's working offices, but it does show the world that in our system of government the independent media are not shut out.

The Dawn of "Managed News"

Although Richard Nixon revolutionized press operations in ways that became permanent fixtures in the White House, John Kennedy's team first turned the corner toward a more sophisticated handling of presidential publicity. It became known as "managed news," a new concept in those days that has now become the routine for how politicians to do business with the media.

Pierre Salinger, Kennedy's press secretary, streamlined and expedited the dissemination of news, but unlike with Nixon, it was not designed to prevent the flow of information. It was to make sure that the president's message was clear and available to reporters. Salinger instituted a "coordinating committee" composed of the chief information officers and government departments. They met once a week.

Salinger's committee became the focal point for press criticism that he was managing or manipulating the news. Today, reporters are so accustomed to this practice that they criticize the White House staff if they are not skilled at managing the news.

The press team that Salinger assembled would review a range of issues, tracking the latest policies and news developments with government agencies and discussing the form and procedure for releasing the content while getting a handle on questions that might come up from reporters covering the administration.

It all seems so quaint in today's world of professional public relations experts guiding politicians in their handling of the media, but in 1960 it was considered out of bounds by some journalists. So much so that the president himself was asked about it in a press conference. Notice how Kennedy uses his famous wit to basically dodge the inquiry from May Craig of the *Portland* (Maine) *Press Herald*:

> **Question:** Mr. President, the practice of managed news is attributed to your administration. Mr. Salinger says he has never had it defined. Would you give us your definition, and tell us why you find it necessary to practice it?
>
> **Kennedy:** You are charging us with something, Mrs. Craig, and then you are asking me to define what it is you are charging me with. I think that you might— Let me just say we've had very limited success in managing the news, if that's what we have been trying to do. Perhaps you would tell us what it is that you object to in our treatment of the news.
>
> **Question:** Are you asking me, sir?
>
> **Kennedy:** Yes.
>
> **Question:** Well, I don't believe in managed news at all. I thought we ought to get everything we want.
>
> **Kennedy:** Well, I think that you should, too, Mrs. Craig. I am for that. [Laughter]

And there you have it. We in the news media think "we ought to get everything we want." That is our nature when it comes to getting information for the public. The suspicion in Kennedy's day was that his team was not just streamlining the release of information, but controlling it. To the extent that that was going on, it was nothing compared to what we experience today.

The working quarters and the nature and size of the press staffs we deal with have dramatically changed since Kennedy's time in office. The White House press corps works in what is now called the James S. Brady Press Briefing Room, named after one of Ronald Reagan's press secretaries. Brady, a genial man who was quite popular with reporters, was permanently disabled by a bullet intended for the president during the assassination attempt that also wounded Reagan.

The briefing room is really a small theater in the West Wing of the White House, hardly big enough for a tiny audience at a school play. It is located between the work space assigned to the White House press corps and the office of the press secretary. What transpires there is sometimes about as amateur and awkward as elementary school kids putting on a holiday show. This is where the press secretary, other government officials, and, occasionally, the president give briefings and take questions. For years these briefings were not televised, but once they were, things changed.

Televised Briefings Are Less Illuminating

The daily give-and-take between reporters and White House spokespeople was more informal—and informative—before television cameras put the show in living rooms around the country. Grandstanding reporters began seeking attention and the officials became even dodgier.

Twice-daily briefings by press secretaries or their assistants began in Dwight Eisenhower's administration and more or less have continued ever since. The big change was in the growing size of the presidential press operation and the press corps itself.

Going back to Franklin Roosevelt's time, a reporter or two could wander by the president's office and, if he was in the mood, engage in some freewheeling banter that might even yield a nugget of news. Such access did not have to be bartered for on arranged days in advance with a committee of aides, as happens today.

Find ways to personally engage at least a few reporters in your press corps, Mr. President. Your aides will tell you otherwise, but it can really help. Not only will you learn a few objective facts about how the outside world views your presidency, but you might even find that the reporting about you gains a bit more context.

Aides will say, "No, no, Mr. President, you can't trust reporters with that kind of access. They're just out to get you." But if you were smart enough to get elected, surely you've got the brains for a give-and-take with journalists that won't get you in trouble.

Richard Nixon closed the era of routine personal encounters between presidents and their reporting entourage. It never came back. He completely transformed presidential press relations, expanded the management structure of the White House press office, and redesigned the space where reporters worked.

It was not just that Nixon intensely disliked the news media more than most presidents and ran against the press in his various campaigns. He had fought the press his entire career and was always seeking to turn the public against them—a tactic many presidents after him also tried. After losing two elections in a row—the 1960 presidential race and his 1962 bid for governor of California—Nixon attacked the media during a stormy news conference.

"You Won't Have Nixon to Kick Around Anymore"

On November 6, 1962, Nixon suffered a humiliating loss for the California governorship to Democrat Edmund "Pat" Brown. The next morning he conceded defeat in one of the bitterest speeches of his political career. Blaming a biased press, Nixon announced that he was leaving politics.

Nixon started this press conference proclaiming that he had "no complaints about the press coverage" of the race he had just lost. "I will never complain about it," Nixon said. "I think that each of you were . . . was . . . writing it as you believed it, and I want that always to be the case in America."

But he could not help himself. Nixon clearly believed the press coverage had been biased in favor of his Democratic opponent. He ended the press conference with a rambling diatribe against the media and a kicker line often replayed through the years.

"You won't have Nixon to kick around anymore," he told the reporters, "because, gentlemen, this is my last press conference."

Nixon's comments leading up to that closing line also should be remembered. He bared his true feelings about the media in a way that many politicians, Democrats and Republicans, would do if they let themselves.

Nixon: My philosophy with regard to the press has never really gotten through. And I want to get it through. This cannot be said for any other American figure today, I guess. Never in my 16 years of campaigning have I complained to a publisher, to an editor, about the coverage of a reporter. I believe a reporter has got a right to write it as he feels it. I believe that if a reporter believes that one man ought to win rather than the other, whether it's on television or radio or the like, he ought to say so. I will say to the reporter sometimes that I think, well, look, I wish you'd give my opponent the same going-over that you give me. And as I leave the press, all that I can say is this: For 16 years, ever since the Hiss case, you've had a lot of fun. A lot of fun. You've had an opportunity to attack me, and I think I've given as good as I've taken.

Despite Nixon's victorious comeback in the 1968 presidential election, his bitterness toward the press did not wane. Relations went from bad to worse during the Watergate scandal.

Press conferences with Nixon grew more and more testy, if not hostile, as the Watergate investigation dragged on. Some of the most famous moments occurred in exchanges with CBS White House correspondent Dan Rather. After one of those incidents, during a March 1974 press conference, Nixon pretty much declared war against the media, if he hadn't already.

Rather: Mr. President, I wonder if you could share with us your thoughts, tell us what goes through your mind when you hear people, people who love this country and people who believe in you, say reluctantly that perhaps you should resign or be impeached?

Nixon: Well, I am glad we don't take the vote of this room, let me say.

The two often sparred. After one testy exchange with his nemesis, Nixon really got personal.

"Are you running for something?" Nixon asked of Rather.

The correspondent's response earned him a permanent spot in the archives of television news:

"Mr. President, are you?"

Although delivered in a respectful tone, Rather's point was clear. Nixon was losing his presidency, despite his recent lopsided reelection. The president was so unpopular that he was running for office all over again, Rather implied.

By that point it was probably too late for Nixon to apply anything that he could learn from press questions, but Rather was telling him things he needed to hear. The country was indeed turning against the president, something he could have seen long before if he had not sealed himself off from exposure to the media.

Years before Watergate overcame Nixon, he had put in place an infrastructure of aides and physical barriers intended to insulate him from the press corps assigned to cover him.

More Aides, Less Openness

A dramatic expansion of White House press handlers in the later decades of the twentieth century did not lead to more openness. In many ways it was like adding more guards in order to prevent prison riots. Direct access to officials throughout the federal government nearly disappeared with the advent of large communications departments charged with managing that access.

In his first year as president, in 1969, Nixon established an entity that survived him in later administrations: the Office of Communications. Suddenly, the White House press office was not just a press secretary and a handful of assistants dedicated to handling reporters in the West Wing. A vastly expanded staff of deputy press secretaries, communications specialists, and others managed a much wider array of publicity efforts aimed at getting around the White House press corps.

The Office of Communications to this day operates in the way Nixon envisioned it—with an even larger staff. It is focused on three types of presidential publicity: out-of-town newspapers and television stations, the specialty press (which later included blogs), and coordination of an ever-growing number of press information officers stationed throughout the executive branch. This infrastructure is not just designed to get the president's message out, but to get it outside of Washington and go over the heads of journalists in the White House.

Nixon's successor, Gerald Ford, further expanded the Office of Communications, as did each president after them, until it grew to have the Leviathan-like status that it has today. The result is that reporters in the White House now rarely see the president without a bureaucratic process that resembles getting a court order, or they only see him at highly structured events such as press conferences.

Gone are the days when a wire reporter once wandered by FDR's office, popped his head in the door and asked, "How old are you, Mr. President?" To which Roosevelt replied, "According to the calendar, my age is sixty-two, but when there is work to be done, I am thirty-five."

Hardly a weighty matter of state, but it is that kind of banter that builds good relations for the big stuff, Mr. President. There must be a way to pierce the wall between you and your press corps without the collapse of the presidency as we know it.

The physical space for working White House reporters was also remodeled under Nixon. To accommodate the growing number of reporters assigned to the White House, Nixon closed the indoor swimming pool, which had been installed by the March of Dimes for Franklin Roosevelt to use for his polio therapy. He covered the pool and built there what would become the briefing room. The swimming pool became a crawl space to handle the wiring of the press operations.

In 2007, the aging Press Briefing Room got a makeover under George W. Bush. While the working area for reporters was remodeled, the most noticeable change was the staging elements of the backdrop for the podium where briefers stand. These changes further established the daily briefings as little more than a television show for burnishing the presidential image.

A softly lit screen behind the podium is flanked by mock columns instead of the blue curtains that once dominated the backdrop. The new podium also contains video screens for teleconferencing and multimedia displays. For safety reasons, the trapdoor that provided access to the old swimming pool (a popular stop for visitors) was replaced by a discreet staircase.

Despite the expense of a two-year construction project and a dramatic face lift, there was one thing that the planners of this remodeling were careful not to do: make room for more reporters. After all that was done, only one more press seat was added to the briefing room.

The last thing presidents want is more reporters to ask more questions that they don't want to hear.

At least the Clintons backed away from the fight that would have ensued if they had followed through with their notion of shrinking our West Wing space. But their other attempt at messing with reporters did erupt in a most public way. As Clinton's team settled into the White House, they did not even put up the pretense of openness that new administrations usually attempt. This was richly symbolized when Clinton's first communications chief, George Stephanopoulos, literally shut the door on White House reporters.

Open the Door!

The press room in the West Wing is adjacent to the press secretary's staff quarters. Reporters were accustomed to being able to walk into the staff area. This is where you could go with a private inquiry that you did not want to ask in front of other reporters at an open briefing—usually because it was a sensitive question that might tip off competitors about what you were working on.

Stephanopoulos had the door to his staff area closed, apparently not understanding how important this access was to us. It seemed to typify the Clinton team's penchant for secrecy and disdain for the media.

Shortly after sealing off his team from us, Stephanopoulos held a televised press briefing that got a bit ugly as reporters piled on, asking, "Why did you close those doors?" What good is having a press secretary if we can't go see the press secretary on an individual basis?

The exchange between Stephanopoulos and the press corps offers a glimpse into how seemingly little things can quickly become a big deal if not handled well. It also represents an ongoing battle between reporters and officials for basic access to public information. Reporters long ago had given up direct access to the president's working area. Now we were fighting for routine access to his communications team.

Question: After one of the most open and inclusive Inaugurals in history he [Pres. Clinton] began his tenure in the White House by limiting access of reporters to parts of the White House Press Office. And, also, do you have plans to further limit such access?

Stephanopoulos: We're reviewing everything right now, but I can say for sure that we're going to be available to answer all of your questions. And we will always be available to answer your questions.

Question: Are you going to continue to block us from going up the steps?

Stephanopoulos: Well, right now we're just trying to figure out how to structure all of the offices upstairs. We're trying to figure out what exactly is the best way to have a good working policy. I mean, there are often changes between administrations. I don't know that the office plans are the same.

Question: Are you going to block us from going up the steps to your office?

Stephanopoulos: We will review any of these kinds of plans with you before we do any—

Question: What does that mean?

Stephanopoulos: That's exactly what it means. We're reviewing everything right now.

Question: But you've done it. You just said you were going to review it with us.

Stephanopoulos: For the time being, we're doing it before we make any permanent decisions. We'll be discussing this with you.

Question: Well, I [Helen] want to tell you that I've been here since Kennedy, and those steps have never been blocked to us, and the Press Secretary's office has never been off-limits. Ever.

Stephanopoulos: The important thing is to make sure you have all the information needed to do your jobs. And that's what we're committed to give.

Question: Well, we don't think that's true.

Question: But that's exactly what you're shutting off, George, is access.

Question: Things happen between briefings.

Question: When you shut the doors, you limit the ability to get information to phone calls and appointments for people in the upper Press Office. Is that the way it's going to be?

Stephanopoulos: First of all, we have not made any final decisions. But I guess I don't fully understand the argument.

Question: We want to knock on your door once in a while when we need it. For example, today is a very good example with the Iraq situation. When that happened, everybody's seeking comment, and we can't get to any of you.

Stephanopoulos: Well, pick up the phone.

Question: We did. The lines were all busy. No calls were returned on that, George.

Stephanopoulos: We'll review everything, and I promise that we'll have access.

Question: What was the reason why you should put upstairs off-limits to us?

Stephanopoulos: Right now we're just going through all of the offices, and we're trying to figure out how to make it work the best.

Question: Well, it's never been done before.

Stephanopoulos: We're just organizing. We're still moving things around.

Question: This has been an open White House for every change of administration. We have automatically assumed that we could get near the press secretary and go upstairs.

Stephanopoulos: And we'll continue to make sure that we can give you all the information you need to do your job.

Although it was a serious matter, during this exchange there were also joking references to Ronald Reagan's famous command at the Berlin Wall—"Mr. Gorbachev, tear down these walls." In effect, we were saying, "Mr. Stephanopoulos, tear down these doors."

Within a couple of days, Stephanopoulos had the contested door opened again.

Stephanopoulos later acknowledged in his book, *All Too Human*, that the closed-door decision was "untenable" and described the episode as a learning experience. Shutting off access to that extent will get you in a fight every time.

"Helen Thomas led the charge," Stephanopoulos wrote. "For more than thirty years she had started her day a little before seven A.M. by planting herself outside the press secretary's office and asking him a question as he walked through the door. Now she couldn't do that anymore. With a voice that sounded then like the Wicked Witch of the West's, she went on the attack. . . . Helen was letting me know who was really in charge. I may have been working for the new president, but she was part of the institutional presidency. She could wait us out, and she intended to win."

While some critics of the media said it was petty for the press corps to make such a spectacle about a closed door, it struck a nerve with many in the public thanks to the whole episode being aired on television. Years later average citizens were still coming up to those of us involved in the incident and asking, "Can you see the press secretary now? Did they ever open those doors?"

It was refreshing that so many in the public understood the symbolism of shutting off the media's access inside the White House. Routine and private entrée to the press secretary and his staff is critical to doing our job, which is to probe beyond the on-the-record briefings and be the public's watchdog.

Mr. President, take responsibility for making sure that your staff handles the press corps in a way that does not lead to an impression that you are avoiding accountability. While the public often gripes about the press, most citizens understand that our role is to hold your feet to the fire on their behalf. Attempts to undermine that role can undermine you.

Too often those hired by the president to be his aides come to think they have become the president themselves. They try to push reporters around, control access, and essentially keep the public in the dark. But they do not just work for the president. They are public servants who get their wages from the taxpayers. They also work for the American people.

Savvy White House aides understand that someday they will not be working for the president, and if they burn too many bridges to reporters while in the West Wing, they could pay a heavy price later in their careers when they might need those contacts. Those who lie to reporters or commit perjury to protect a president pay the heaviest price of all—and are often abandoned by the president they served at all cost.

Nixon's henchmen, H. R. Haldeman and John Daniel Ehrlichman, were actually fired when their unlawful activities became public even though they were doing the president's bidding. It is not unusual for a president to show no mercy for those who were actually ordered to do things that ultimately got them in trouble. White House aides should always remember that the fact that the president is the one telling them to do something does not make it right or legal.

A Wild Chase

Presidents love secrecy. Sometimes it is downright comical.

Lyndon Johnson, for instance, considered it great sport to stiff-arm the press. One Sunday near the president's ranch in Texas, Helen and other journalists were following his motorcade in a press vehicle on a routine trip to church. Suddenly, Johnson ordered his driver to speed up and ditch the media car.

A wild chase ensued. The press car eventually caught up with Johnson at the entrance to the church. He was standing outside enjoying a hearty laugh at the ruckus he had caused.

Still, Johnson was one of the most accessible presidents in modern times for reporters covering his White House. But most of what he told us he wanted kept off the record or unattributed to him. Despite that compromise, Johnson's many private sessions with groups of reporters allowed them to understand his thinking about issues of the day and do a more accurate job of reporting to the public.

Much of Johnson's courting of the press was aimed at gaining our sympathy. He really felt sorry for himself much of the time. "I'm the only president you've got," he would say when fretting about how things were going for him. Occasionally he seemed almost jealous of our constitutional protections, saying, "You all have the First Amendment," as though it was our private preserve that we used as a special weapon against presidents.

Like most presidents, Johnson felt the press was against him at times and trying to do him in. At his core, LBJ wanted to be loved. It was sad to see him become so personally unpopular as the Vietnam War unraveled his presidency. He was obsessed with wanting everyone to love him. He wanted to be on the front page every day with his best foot forward. By the end of his time in office he was on the front page all right—and it was all bad news for him, no matter how much he courted us.

Had his war decisions not gone so badly, Johnson's eagerness to give reporters personal access to him would have served him well. But the world collapsing around him could not be changed by privately arguing his case to the press.

Mr. President, take this lesson from Lyndon Johnson's press dealings. Let us in. As bad as things got for him, his legacy over time is being restored thanks to the many reporters who understood him and tempered some of the harsh feelings against him—all because he really talked to us.

Johnson was a man who had to talk. He was extraordinarily garrulous. He let us in and we saw him agonizing over Vietnam. He did not hide it from us.

It was a unique moment for a president to take a reporter aside and really tell you what was bothering him. Yet despite his openness, Johnson was also self-protective. "Now, you know, that's off the record," he would say after telling you his innermost feelings. But we knew the game. He really wanted us to write what we were hearing, but not attribute it to him.

Other times, Johnson would gather a group of reporters for one of his impromptu press conferences. They could be physically grueling. He would gather his beagles and call on us to join his famously fast-paced walk, circling the South Lawn many times. Now, these were the days of high heels and pointed toes, so it was agonizing to try to keep up with the presidential dog walk, ask questions, and take notes. We called it our version of the Bataan Death March.

To make it worse, Johnson would speak almost in a whisper so that we had to bunch up as close to him as possible to hear what he was saying. It was almost sadistic. But no matter the conditions, any time a president gives the press access to his thinking, we will tag along without complaint.

Don't Hide, Mr. President

Give Johnson's methods a try, Mr. President. Don't hide behind aides or rely solely on formal televised press conferences to interact with the news media. Give reporters access to your thinking in a meaningful way, even if you must do it privately. Sure, you might get burned now and then if a reporter violates a ground rule about attributing something to you. Just don't talk to that reporter again. You will find that nearly to a person the White House reporters will abide by your rules in order to keep the access.

Sadly, a rising wall has been built between presidents and the White House press corps since Johnson. Presidents now routinely dodge the media. And the more distance between the president and the reporters who cover him, the more antagonistic the relationship—creating still more distance. Nowadays, the avoidance of the press begins even before the president is sworn in.

Reporters Wimp Out

As the game of keep-away became the norm, reporters became less insistent on getting access to the candidate or the president. There was a time when the news media would become so unruly—and surly in their coverage—that they were able to force press availabilities. But such feistiness has been ground out of the press corps over the years.

Much of the coverage of candidates or presidents is now limited to reporting their speeches, which they seldom write for themselves. Most of the questions they take are generally from friendly audiences in town hall settings. These sessions produce a tiny bit of real dialogue, but are often limited to memorized sound bites in response to predictable questions.

For gleaning something new or revealing, there is no substitute for an independent press able to ask unexpected questions. Sure, it might not always serve the president's interests, but it does serve the public's right to know.

The Rewards of Openness

A president who is comfortable and engaging with the press corps, even while under fire, will always come across as more open and responsive. It encourages confidence in your competence, Mr. President, and helps you avoid the image of an imperial presidency.

John F. Kennedy was the first president to hold live televised press conferences. He set a standard for success that has seldom been matched. His wit and his warmth in good-natured bantering with reporters captured the imagination of the American people. They began watching with great interest, enjoying the sight of a president in an unrehearsed setting, speaking in his own words.

It was clear that Kennedy enjoyed these sessions. He knew how to handle the press, deflect a tough question with a joke, and generally disarm the press corps if the questions began going in a direction he might not like.

Kennedy's press conferences were critical to his growing popularity. They can be for any president, unless handled with suspicion and dread. Kennedy never seemed afraid of being unprepared, confident that he could wing it if necessary. He walked into the room with a genuine smile, without a hint of the arrogance of power that some presidents brought to these encounters. Of course, Kennedy knew he could knock us down with a witty remark if he had to—and he often did. Rarely did Kennedy show anger at questions he didn't like. But he was not above it. He once became visibly upset at a silly question insinuating that there were communists in his government. Despite moments like that, he never viewed the press as his enemy.

Sometimes presidents do get oddball questions. These are usually opportunities, not challenges. More often than not, they set up a moment for the president to show a little humor—or maybe even a flash of anger that proves he is human.

Franklin Roosevelt was well known for not suffering fools gladly when questioned by the press. If he didn't like a question, he'd order the reporter to go stand in the corner. But at least he took questions, unlike those who try to ignore the media.

Some presidents could be a tad creative when handling questions they did not like. Once, after inviting two reporters to ride with him in his limousine, Johnson got a question about his least favorite topic of the day. He was asked about rumors that Robert F. Kennedy was considering a presidential run. This was before Johnson had announced he would not run for reelection in 1968, which meant that RFK would be challenging the president for his own party's nomination.

"Do you like these cuff links?" Johnson responded, holding the presidential wrist up for the reporters to observe. Clearly, he was not going to comment, which oftentimes is an answer unto itself. Johnson's terse deflection tended to confirm the irritation we knew he felt about Robert Kennedy's ambitions.

Even a "No comment" or a creative equivalent is better than refusing to be asked a difficult question, Mr. President. When you must stall to think of an answer, or dodge a question altogether, learn to do so with the style and sophistication that Kennedy commanded and you can get away with it.

Americans liked Kennedy's presentations because he made them entertaining and they could understand what he was saying. Most important, they felt he was telling the truth, even when he was not really answering the question.

Openness Is Trustworthy

It is a matter of trust. When presidents do not trust the public to handle the truth, more often than not it comes back to haunt them. In many cases, more openness to questions allows a skilled president to make a better case to the public. This is especially true when the public is already asking tough questions.

Failing to bring the public and Congress along for the ride can leave you helpless if you make mistakes, Mr. President. When nearly everyone in the country is questioning your decisions, you had better answer the questions with humility and honesty. Americans can be quite forgiving unless you stubbornly deny that anything is wrong.

For example, Kennedy's first instinct was to dodge questions about the disastrous Bay of Pigs episode, when an American-backed invasion of communist Cuba failed miserably. Initially, he thought it would be inappropriate to discuss it, saying it served no national purpose. Naturally, he was trying to save his own skin. But he was also smart enough to quickly realize that the questions had to be answered, because the public was asking them, whether or not it served the national purpose.

When Kennedy took full responsibility for the debacle and publicly acknowledged the failure, his poll standings improved. People thought, well, that's very big of him, very courageous. Indeed, Kennedy's mea culpa was so successful that it became something of a gold standard for politicians in trouble. So much so that it has become a cliché to quickly take responsibility when things go wrong.

Question Time

Congress does not duplicate the British Parliament's "Question Time," when the prime minister endures often hostile inquiries from the opposing party. While our presidents would be loath to submit to such ordeals, it might actually be a good idea. It certainly seems to help those British prime ministers who can skillfully handle their opponents' questions and reassure their citizens that they do not consider themselves above it all.

The equivalent in the United States may be the need to ask follow-up questions during press conferences. Voters should pay close attention when presidents or their aides refuse to allow them. These are often the moments when they are trying to dodge the truth.

The follow-up question is a crucial part of getting information that the people have a right to know. Often that first answer is a dodge, an attempt to stick to a talking point or a scripted answer. Only by asking the follow-up question can evasive answers be explored.

Most presidents since Calvin Coolidge have allowed reporters to ask a second question based on the answer to the first. In fact, George W. Bush was the first since Coolidge to rule them out of order except on rare occasions.

Demonizing the Messenger

The last refuge of a failing president, after dodging media questions and giving speeches that fall flat, is to dispatch aides and pundit friends to attack the press in a pathetic attempt to play the martyr. Even when they are riding high in the polls, presidents and their staff try to blame the media when tough questions are asked.

At a White House press briefing on March 18, 2003, at the outset of the Iraq War, Bush press secretary Ari Fleischer repeated the blame-the-questioner technique in an exchange with Helen. It was something he had deployed many times when asked about the impending invasion.

> **Helen:** Does it bother the President that most of the world is against this war?
> **Fleischer:** Helen, this is an issue where you and I will never agree when you state your premise about what the people think.
> **Helen:** This isn't you and I. This is a very legitimate question.

Fleischer then interrupted an attempt to cite accounts of foreign leaders, members of the United Nations, and surveys showing significant opposition to an immediate war in Iraq.

"I understand your strong opinions clearly," Fleischer said. "I'm not sure the American people agree with you."

Instead of answering the question, Fleischer made the reporter the issue. And yet so many Americans watching at home would have asked such a question. It was important for the White House to explain why we were going to war. They were bragging in great detail about how we were going to drop bombs, but they didn't want to give clear answers about the reasons for the war.

Fleischer's handling of scrutiny about Iraq is typical of what has become a refined method for politicians facing unpleasant or difficult questions from reporters. Make the reporters the issue by accusing them of bias. Demonizing the messenger is what presidents and their teams often do when they prefer not to directly respond to the message.

It is almost always the case that a White House obsessively on the attack against the news media does not represent an administration dedicated to openness. It should be the first clue for voters that the White House is a closed shop.

FIVE

TELL THE TRUTH: YOU'LL BE FORGIVEN

Let the people know the facts, and the country will be safe.
—ABRAHAM LINCOLN

Presidents and their image makers are notoriously prone to exaggeration, or worse. Sometime they outright lie. But more often than not it pays to tell the truth, Mr. President.

Being honest gets presidents *out* of trouble.

Ronald Reagan was almost impeached for the Iran-Contra scandal that overtook his second term—until he went on television to address the nation and tell the truth, acknowledging an arms-for-hostages deal that his administration also used to fund Nicaraguan Contras.

Telling hard truths makes great leaders.

Abraham Lincoln was the first president to take on slavery and tell the nation it was wrong. His immediate predecessors had done all they could to dodge the issue in order to keep slave states in the Union.

Sometimes being truthful is about jarring the nation into a better mood. Franklin Roosevelt led the country out of economic depression by urging citizens to overcome their fear.

Honesty often means taking on powerful interests, as when Dwight Eisenhower bluntly warned against giving too much power to the "military industrial complex." Or when Grover Cleveland stood up to railroad barons. And when Theodore Roosevelt busted business monopolies that were strangling the nation's economy.

Great presidents tell the truth when it's difficult, not just when it's easy.

"The Very Word 'Secrecy' Is Repugnant in a Free and Open Society"

At the peak of the Cold War, John F. Kennedy took the podium at a convention of the American Newspaper Publishers Association in New York City to give a remarkable speech that in many ways finally put an end to a long period of assaults on individual rights in the name of fighting communism.

"There is very grave danger that an announced need for increased security will be seized upon by those anxious to expand its meaning to the very limits of official censorship and concealment," Kennedy said in April of 1961 just a few months after becoming president.

Although one of Kennedy's lesser-known speeches today, it was widely covered at the time and served to bring about a change that was long overdue. It was a prime example of presidential bravery in using the truth to change popular opinion.

Kennedy's presidency followed a long period of reactionary anti-communist hysteria that had gripped the nation. This era was most famously symbolized by the witch hunts of Senator Joe McCarthy (R-Wis.) and other sordid attempts by politicians to victimize innocents accused of being "un-American."

By taking a firm and honest stand against such tyranny, Kennedy put the country back on a path toward its roots as a more open and democratic society. The admirable thing about Kennedy's choice is how what he did was in some ways against his own interests. A president in those times could have enhanced his own power, silenced his critics, and bullied his foes by taking advantage of the public's willingness to forgo their rights to fight communism.

Instead, in this speech Kennedy invited the criticism that comes with an open society, vowing that he would not tolerate anyone in his government, civilian or military, using a war against communism to "censor the news, to stifle dissent, to cover up our mistakes or to withhold from the press and the public the facts they deserve to know."

Kennedy's words on that night at the Waldorf-Astoria should be a constant reminder to all future presidents about the need to hold true to our values as a nation, especially when we face threats from those who would harm us:

> The very word "secrecy" is repugnant in a free and open society; and we are as a people inherently and historically opposed to secret societies, to secret oaths and to secret proceedings. We decided long ago that the dangers of excessive and unwarranted concealment of pertinent facts far outweighed the dangers which are cited to justify it. Even today, there is little value in opposing the threat of a closed society by imitating its arbitrary restrictions. Even today, there is little value in insuring the survival of our nation if our traditions do not survive with it.

"Mr. Gorbachev, Tear Down This Wall!"

A bit of unwelcome honesty aimed at another country is sometimes a president's job.

Ronald Reagan seized such a moment in 1987 at the Brandenburg Gate near the Berlin Wall, putting severe pressure on Soviet leader Mikhail Gorbachev to allow his own citizens the freedom to travel outside their borders.

"General Secretary Gorbachev, if you seek peace, if you seek prosperity for the Soviet Union and eastern Europe, if you seek liberalization, come here to this gate," Reagan said. "Mr. Gorbachev, open this gate. Mr. Gorbachev, tear down this wall!"

And twenty-nine months later Gorbachev did just that, allowing Berliners to destroy the wall. Former West German chancellor Helmut Kohl later said he would never forget standing near Reagan when he challenged Gorbachev. "He was a stroke of luck for the world, especially for Europe."

President Barack Obama also tried some tough and direct candor aimed at the citizens of a hostile nation in a videotaped address to the people of Iran, a country that has been at the top of presidential enemies' lists for more than thirty years.

"With the coming of a new season, we're reminded of this precious humanity that we all share," Obama said to Iranians early in his presidency. "And we can once again call upon this spirit as we seek the promise of a new beginning. This process will not be advanced by threats. We seek instead engagement that is honest and grounded in mutual respect. The United States wants the Islamic Republic of Iran to take its rightful place in the community of nations. You have that right—but it comes with real responsibilities."

"The Real Truth of Our Lives"

Ultimately, it is up to America's citizens to demand truth from our presidents. We must not make them politically afraid to tell us what we do not want to hear.

It is important to recognize, appreciate, and reward a president who is brave enough to tell us hard truths. But to do that we must be a truthful, discerning society, honest with ourselves and prepared to "doubt our own infallibility," as Benjamin Franklin once advised to bitterly opposed camps at the Constitutional Convention.

We must give presidents the space to be honest without rebuke, especially when they challenge conventional wisdom. Democracy is dependent upon facts, not ideology. Partisan hypocrites who spin every situation to their advantage are perverting our civic life.

When British playwright Harold Pinter received his Nobel Prize for literature in 2005, he delivered a lecture that serves as a manifesto for the responsibility of all citizens to insist upon truthful leadership:

"I believe that despite the enormous odds which exist, unflinching, unswerving, fierce intellectual determination, as citizens, to define the real truth of our lives and our societies is a crucial obligation which devolves upon us all," Pinter said. "It is in fact mandatory. If such a determination is not embodied in our political vision we have no hope of restoring what is so nearly lost to us—the dignity of man."

"We Must Face the Truth"

Unfortunately, there are times when honorable presidents tell us the truth and we don't listen. Jimmy Carter was such a president. He tried to warn the nation about dependence on foreign oil, for instance. Had Americans heeded his call for conserving energy and developing alternative fuel sources, perhaps we would not have felt the need to conduct wars in the Persian Gulf years after he left office.

Carter's seminal truth-telling moment came on the night of July 15, 1979, in one of the most remarkable nationally televised speeches ever given by a president. After ten days of closed-door meetings at Camp David with leaders from throughout the country, President Carter delivered what became known as his "Malaise Speech."

The nation was facing many troubles. A gas shortage, the result of manipulation by foreign oil producers, had led to long lines at the pump. Inflation was on the rise. And the public was as cynical about their government as ever.

Although the word "malaise" was not in Carter's text, it became the emblem on his unusually candid description of how he viewed the emotional condition of the country. No president before or since Carter has talked so directly and emotionally to the American people in quite this way:

> I want to speak to you tonight about . . . a fundamental threat to American democracy. . . . The threat is nearly invisible in ordinary ways. It is a crisis of confidence. It is a crisis that strikes at the very heart and soul and spirit of our national will. We can see this crisis in the growing doubt about the meaning of our own lives and in the loss of a unity of purpose for our nation. . . . Our people are

losing faith, not only in government itself but in the ability as citizens to serve as the ultimate rulers and shapers of our democracy.... Human identity is no longer defined by what one does, but by what one owns.... The symptoms of this crisis of the American spirit are all around us.... Two-thirds of our people do not even vote. The productivity of American workers is actually dropping, and the willing-ness of Americans to save for the future has fallen below that of all other people in the Western world.... The gap between our citizens and our government has never been so wide. The people are looking for honest answers, clear leadership, not false claims and evasiveness and politics as usual. We must face the truth, and then we can change our course. We simply must have faith in each other, faith in our ability to govern ourselves, and faith in the future of this nation.

Few presidents were ever so blunt about the nation's ills. Most prefer to pretend that things are just fine. But the most exceptional aspect of this speech was Carter's suggestion that the American peo-ple might bear some responsibility for their problems.

What a concept! A president saying the American people are less than perfect. That departure from the glowing praise that presidents usually heap upon their subjects stands alone in the annals of White House history.

It was a phenomenal gamble for Carter to appear on television with such harsh truths, griping about the public's foul mood and telling them to get up and do something about it. But perhaps this was a case of a president delivering too much bitter medicine. Instead of getting credit for leveling with the public, Carter was blamed for causing the very malaise that he had described. He never really lived it down. During the 2004 presidential campaign, Vice President Dick Cheney warned that Democratic nominee John Kerry would return the nation to the "malaise" of the Carter era.

Yet Carter's honesty paid dividends in the years after his presi-dency. The American people ultimately came to see him as an earnest and honest man. Many eventually realized they should have listened to his warnings in the 1970s about the painful consequences of our cavalier ways, which came true just a few decades later.

Mr. President, when you tell the truth, you might not be forgiven while you're in office. But one day you will be. It's still worth it to tell hard truths.

An honest president might not always be appreciated during his term of duty. If you are telling the truth, however, your legacy will rise above the dark days. And in the end, your eventual legacy is more important to your place in history than what the voters thought during your time in office.

"I Can Only Be as Factual as the Facts Permit"

The business of becoming president is now much changed from Washington's experience. Reluctant heroes are passed over. Fiercely ambitious self-promoters win elections, even as they feign modesty.

Truth does not count for much in our politics. Believable spin is valued more than the right policy. But while so much in our society is dramatically changing, certain principles never do. Truth is above all. Without honest government, democracy is perverted.

Credibility is everything for a president. The American people want to believe what a president says. Therefore, it takes a long time, and many lies, for a president to lose that credibility. And when the country loses faith in your honesty, Mr. President, you will never get it back. Telling a lie might work for the moment, but if you get caught before you confess, your presidency will crumble around you.

The Greek tragedy of Richard Nixon's downfall was more about the public losing faith in his basic honesty. Once that was gone, there was no way on God's green earth to put Humpty Dumpty back together again—and Nixon and his staff tried everything. In a hilarious attempt at pseudo-candor during a briefing, Nixon's press secretary Ron Ziegler said, "I can only be as factual as the facts permit."

Too often, presidents or their aides try to fix the facts, making adjustments to the truth according to what they think the public wants to hear. Then, once they think the public is ready for the full truth, they let it out.

"I Did Not Have Sexual Relations with That Woman"

Bill Clinton believed that he had to slowly let the truth out or be drummed out of office when the nation learned about his sexual affair with White House intern Monica Lewinsky.

Speaking to reporters in the Roosevelt Room of the White House on January 26, 1998, Clinton faced a perilous time as newspaper headlines screamed the sordid news:

"A CRISIS WITH NO PARALLEL," *The Washington Post*
"WHITE HOUSE ACTS TO CONTAIN FUROR AS CONCERN
  GROWS," *The New York Times*
"CLINTON FIGHTS TO SAVE HIS PRESIDENCY," *Chicago Tribune*
"EX-INTERN ACCUSED OF TRYST WITH PRESIDENT," *Los Angeles
  Times*

Five days earlier, shortly after popping up on the Internet, the name "Monica S. Lewinsky" became media fodder. The newspapers reported that the twenty-four-year-old former White House intern was being questioned by prosecutors about allegations that she and Clinton had an affair, and that he encouraged her to lie under oath in a civil lawsuit deposition.

In the days leading up to his Roosevelt Room appearance, Clinton had tried to dodge and parse without directly lying. He told PBS anchor Jim Lehrer that there was no "improper relationship." Pressed for an explanation, he said, "There is no sexual relationship."

Why had the president limited this remark to the present tense? reporters asked White House aides. They were well-schooled in paying close attention to Clinton's words. He had a history of carefully choosing words with a literal meaning that could be quite different from the impression he wished to give. The technical meaning of Clinton's phrasing—"there is no sexual relationship"—was as limited as it could be. He was only saying that he wasn't in a relationship at the time of the interview, which was true.

Second-guessing the president's limited denials produced even more buzz in the White House press room. It was a full-scale frenzy. Reporters hounded Clinton's staff. When would he directly address the American people about this?

As Clinton began to speak in the Roosevelt Room on January 26, a *Washington Post* poll just published showed that 57 percent of the Americans surveyed thought Clinton did indeed have the affair with an intern, and 36 percent thought he should resign because of it.

Clinton's fear, shared by his pollsters, was that it was too soon to admit the relationship and ask for forgiveness. He felt the public needed more time to think this over and get used to the idea that their president had behaved so poorly. Clinton's lawyers also argued against a contrition strategy. They feared that independent prosecutor Kenneth Starr would pounce, perhaps even file criminal charges against the president.

What Clinton said about Lewinsky that day took only twenty seconds and sixty-two words—and became one of the most oft-repeated clips of his presidency. And he had chosen to lie.

"I want to say one thing to the American people," Clinton said. "I want you to listen to me. I'm going to say this again. I did not have sexual relations with that woman, Miss Lewinsky. I never told anybody to lie, not a single time—never. These allegations are false. And I need to go back to work for the American people."

Clinton's body language suggested he might not be telling the truth. The Associated Press report noted how he "paused twice and licked his lips." He "glanced left, right and down, but not once did he make eye contact with the reporters or camera lenses watching intently from the back of the room."

Even by Washington's narrowly drawn definition of lying, this was a whopper. It might not have been a lie about anything that should have mattered. No one had died. The Constitution was not threatened. The president having sex was hardly something that would bring the country down. But there was no escaping, parsing, or misinterpreting Clinton's words on that day. He flat-out lied.

This was much more than spin, Washington's gentle word for lies. The consensus definition of lying is so tightly drawn in our politics that bald-faced lies become truth.

What is a lie? One simple definition is any intent to deceive. If that were our definition in Washington, we would be slapping on the label a lot more often. Still, it would be better to have a broad definition for lying, even if it results in more violations. Otherwise, you get the slippery slope that we are on now.

These days, only when a president knowingly and completely denies the truth, as Clinton did about Lewinsky, are we inclined to call it a lie. Sometimes spin really is something less than a lie. But even if the precise words are truthful, the spinner's intent to deceive makes it a lie.

Deceitfully spinning the truth is so common and expected in Washington that politicians often go off the record when they want to tell a reporter the truth. What does that tell you?

Twisting the truth has gotten so perverse in Washington that few believe a quote if it is said in public. But if it is said off the record as an anonymous quote, it rings true.

Presidents sometimes lie because we reward them for it. Clinton might have been right that admitting his affair with Lewinsky too soon would have produced unbearable pressure to resign. During an appearance on NBC's *Today Show* at the time, First Lady Hillary Rodham Clinton had to dodge a question about the prospect of her husband resigning if the affair really happened.

"Trouble—big time," NBC's Tim Russert said in an interview during the days leading up to Clinton's Roosevelt Room speech. "His closest friends are telling me he will not survive this if he lied and perjured himself and asked someone else to perjure themselves. . . . This is so devastating."

Such talk waned a bit after Clinton so firmly asserted his innocence, but did that lie really save his presidency from a quick death? It did give him cover while he waited for the public to get used to the truth about his scandalous White House affair. But once the lie was exposed, it made Clinton's problems worse.

Clinton's belief that Americans were not ready for the facts recalls the words of Jack Nicholson's character, Colonel Nathan R. Jessup, in the courtroom thriller *A Few Good Men*. Accused of giving an order that leads to a marine's death, Nicholson defends his actions as a necessary evil. When the prosecutor, played by Tom Cruise, says, "I want the truth," Nicholson's character famously responds, "You can't handle the truth."

We cannot know whether the country could have handled the truth when Clinton originally lied about Lewinsky. He did not give us a chance.

It is also possible that if Clinton had been honest in the beginning he might not have faced House impeachment and a Senate trial. It was Clinton's intransigence and scorched-earth tactics that seemed to fuel much of that movement.

It was, after all, the lying—in court and in public—that got him impeached, that distracted his presidency so. The lingering scandal probably robbed Clinton, a talented and brilliant leader, of any chance to do great things.

"Read My Lips"

Is breaking a campaign promise a lie? When circumstances fundamentally change, Americans can be quite forgiving about your going back on your word, Mr. President. But it's a different story when they suspect you never meant to keep the promise in the first place.

It was on taxes that George H. W. Bush told what turned out to be one of the most famous untruths in presidential politics. "Read my lips, no new taxes," candidate Bush said in his successful 1988 bid. As president, he agreed to higher taxes and lost crucial support among conservatives, paving the way for Clinton to beat him in 1992.

In that campaign, Clinton refined the tax fib. He promised not to raise taxes "to pay for new programs." He later pushed the biggest tax increase in U.S. history through Congress, insisting that he had kept his campaign pledge because the higher taxes only paid for old programs. But there is no escaping that he intended voters in 1992 to believe that he would not raise taxes at all.

George H. W. Bush foisted a lesser-known lie upon the nation in the ridiculous episode of the so-called Drug War. Speaking to the nation from the Oval Office in 1989, he held up a plastic bag filled with a white chunky substance.

"This is crack cocaine," Bush sternly announced, claiming that it was "seized a few days ago in a park across the street from the White House. . . . It could easily have been heroin or PCP."

But it turned out to be a setup. Drug Enforcement Administration (DEA) agents had struggled to lure a drug dealer to nearby Lafayette Park for the sole purpose of creating a dramatic prop for the president's speech. A DEA agent later told the *Washington Post* that the agency faced considerable difficulty in obtaining the crack to match the words of Bush's speechwriters. Four days before the speech was given, an undercover DEA agent posing as a drug buyer persuaded an eighteen-year-old drug dealer to meet him at the park across the street from the White House.

"Where the [expletive] is the White House?" the high school senior replied in a conversation that was secretly tape-recorded by the DEA. When told it was the residence of the president, he replied, "Oh, you mean where Reagan lives." The dealer found his way to Lafayette Park and the president's prop was secured.

"We had to manipulate him to get him down there," DEA agent William McMullan told the *Post.* "It wasn't easy." The DEA agent paid $2,400 for three ounces of crack later delivered to the West Wing.

A few days later, when the ruse became public, Bush defended what his staff and the DEA had done.

"I think it was great because it sent a message to the United States that even across from the White House they can sell drugs," Bush said. "Every time that some guy gets caught selling drugs, he pleads that somebody is luring [him] someplace."

Bush's son, George W., outdid his father in the lying department on far graver matters. He built a case for war on what turned out to be false pretenses—that Iraqi dictator Saddam Hussein possessed weapons of mass destruction. Those claims helped justify the 2003 invasion of Iraq, but long after the first phase of combat had ended, the second Bush administration finally acknowledged they never had the proof they had claimed. By then, 140,000 U.S. troops were stuck in Iraq. More than 4,000 had died. Civilian casualties, while not "officially" tallied, were in the tens of thousands.

Spinning the evidence for war, whether it is a domestic drug war or a foreign invasion, is truly beyond the pale for presidents. The danger of the modern terrorist threat is that the more unconventional and unidentifiable our enemies are, the easier it is to imagine ourselves into war. When we can't really see foes who might be hiding in caves, we can be drawn into a state of perpetual war.

Have we learned the real truths about what our government knew about the terrorist threat before the September 11, 2001, attacks on our soil? Attempts to suppress information about mistakes and oversights only deny us the opportunity to be more effective in stopping future attacks.

Not fully understanding terrorism itself is a form of denying truth that makes us less safe. Finding a better way of stopping terrorism begins with considering some hard truths, such as the role of what many see as American imperialism in fostering hatred of our nation.

We must get back to a world that sees America as a beacon of democracy. The great promise of our country is to be a vehicle for improving the lot of all mankind.

We cannot fulfill that promise in a system where so many politicians think it is all right to lie—while the news media look the other way.

"Presidents Have a Right to Lie"

A top Kennedy administration official once said, "Presidents have a right to lie." Even the man who said it—Assistant Secretary of Defense Arthur Sylvester—later backed away from his comment. But presidents and their aides so often come to believe just that.

When one lie seems justified, the next several become easier. And before you know it, Mr. President, your administration is built on lies, which can be very confusing. Former senator George Aiken (R-Vt.) once noted, "If you don't lie, you don't have to remember what you said."

The danger for an administration that piles on the lies is that you never know who might spill the beans. Of all the strange ways that the truth came out in Nixon's Watergate meltdown, one of the oddest sources was the colorful wife of one of his own cabinet members. Her honesty with reporters behind the scenes put many of us on the path to the light in a very dark tunnel.

Publicly, Martha Mitchell was almost a cartoon character, her vivaciousness and blunt talk coming across as a bit nutty when chopped up into sound bites and pithy quotes. Once on a trip aboard Air Force One, while her husband, Attorney General John Mitchell, was in a meeting with Nixon, Martha got bored and wandered into the press area.

After demanding that reporters ask her "something important," Mrs. Mitchell was asked, "What do you think of the Vietnam War?"

"It stinks," she said, launching a full-throated rant against the war. Later, we asked her husband if he would like to hear what she had said. "Heavens no," the attorney general answered. "I might have to jump out the window."

Once the Nixon team got word of Mitchell's remarks, her husband said he would only allow his wife to give interviews in Swahili.

That episode, while laughingly dismissed as "crazy Martha," turned out to be somewhat prophetic as she ended up being a source in the Watergate scandal that contributed to the downfall of the Nixon White House and her own husband.

Later, as Martha closely observed her husband, who had left the cabinet to direct Nixon's 1972 reelection bid, she began putting together the pieces of Watergate, always suspecting that the break-in at the Democratic headquarters was much more than a third-rate burglary. She turned out to be right in believing that high crimes were being committed. Her late-night calls to reporters provided many clues that bore fruit.

After her death from bone cancer in 1976, Martha Mitchell's funeral featured a telling wreath with flowers that spelled out the message "Martha was right."

Cover-Ups Don't Work Forever

You never know how you might get caught if you lie too much, Mr. President. With 4 million government workers in your employ, even the lowliest bureaucrat can open the floodgates against you.

Linda Tripp, a low-level defense department employee, happened to become acquainted with Monica Lewinsky when both worked in the Pentagon public affairs office, and became the younger woman's confidante. She later learned of the young intern's affair with Bill Clinton, and conspired with the president's political enemies to out the story.

Beware the cover-up if your lies catch up with you, Mr. President. Since Watergate, it has become one of Washington's most oft-repeated truisms that it's always the cover-up that gets them. The list just keeps getting longer: Reagan's Iran-Contra scandal, Clinton's Lewinsky debacle, George W. Bush's CIA leak case. Over and over, administrations instinctively compound their lies, once uncovered, with more lies that get them into even more trouble.

In many cases, presidents save themselves once they fess up and seek forgiveness. The American people can be so forgiving, Mr. President, unless you cross that final line of credibility and keep the lies in play long after anyone believes you.

Why are we so forgiving of our presidents? For starters, we elected them. Deciding that our president is a crook and a liar means that we have to admit to ourselves that our own judgment was in error. Therefore, the evidence has to become overwhelming for most voters to make that journey.

Also, we simply want to believe in our presidents. They symbolize our hopes and ideals, and how we want to be seen by the rest of the world. Without monarchs to worship, we invest in our presidents the passion of followers who yearn for a great leader.

"Too True to Be Doubted"

White House image makers feed the public's inner desire to believe their presidents. The trappings of office—be they images of the president on Air Force One or a phalanx of flags behind a podium—are all used to show authority and command confidence.

The "Father of Our Country" myth is deeply ingrained and easily fed by crafty professionals. It goes back to George Washington himself, whose reputation for self-sacrifice, honesty, and wisdom set the standard for all presidents to come.

Yet it turns out that a wildly popular story, retold for generations as proof of Washington's lifelong commitment to truth, was almost certainly a lie made up by a man who might very well have been the first presidential image maker. Historians are convinced that an overly exuberant biographer, Mason Locke Weems, made up the story of Washington, at age six, supposedly confessing to his father that he chopped down a cherry tree.

The flamboyant title of Weems's 1809 book containing the cherry tree tale might be a clue that it did not contain the unvarnished truth: *A History of the Life and Death, Virtues and Exploits of General George Washington: With Curious Anecdotes Equally Honorable to Himself and Exemplary.*

The story in Weems's book, which the author dubbed "too true to be doubted," goes like this:

> "George," said his father, "do you know who killed that beautiful little cherry tree yonder in the garden?" This was a tough question; and George staggered under it for a moment; but quickly recovered himself: and looking at his father, with the sweet face of youth brightened with the inexpressible charm of all-conquering truth, he bravely cried out, "I can't tell a lie, Pa; you know I can't tell a lie. I did cut it with my hatchet." "Run to my arms, you dearest boy," cried his father, "run to my arms; glad am I, George, that you killed my tree; for you have paid me for it a thousand fold. Such an act of heroism in my son is more worth than a thousand trees, though blossomed with silver, and their fruits of purest gold."

The story was never independently verified. Nor was Weems's claim that young Washington was so strong that he threw a silver dollar across the Potomac River. The river is a mile wide at the point where Washington supposedly accomplished this feat, and there were no silver dollars when he was that young.

The author's description of his anonymous source for these anecdotes is less than convincing: "An aged lady, who was a distant relative, and, when a girl, spent much of her time in the family."

Whether or not it was true, the story was retold to generations of American children when learning life lessons about the "Father of Our Country." Archaeologists even looked for signs of cherry trees or hatchets in 2008 when the remains of Washington's childhood home were finally discovered at Ferry Farm, just across the Rappahannock River from Fredericksburg, Virginia. They did not find any clues.

Like many aggrandizing stories about our presidents, the cherry-tree tale is really a parable, a simple story to illustrate what we want to believe—that Washington was wise, honorable, and true even as a six-year-old. The various myths and truths that elevated Washington in his times became a model for how so many of his successors wish to be seen.

By all accounts, George Washington apparently was a truthful man. Had Weems written the cherry-tree fable while Washington was alive, the nation's first president probably would have repudiated the story.

This just goes to show how lying about presidents happens even after they are long gone. We simply want to believe that our presidents are better than ourselves, even if deep down we know that they are just human beings with the usual number of flaws.

Let's face it. Despite all evidence to the contrary, we still want to believe that a six-year-old George Washington really did tell the truth about that cherry tree.

SIX

HAVE COURAGE:
EVEN IF IT HURTS

Once they feel the heat, they'll see the light.
—LYNDON JOHNSON

There are several different ways in which our presidents have displayed courage—or the lack of it. Some ways are better than others. Be courageous when it helps, Mr. President. Other times it might be best to back down.

For political courage, there is showing leadership against the grain—doing or saying what's good for the country even if it costs you support from the voters and other politicians. Think about Lyndon Johnson's railroading civil rights legislation through Congress while knowing full well that it would undermine his own political party's future in the segregated South.

"One man with courage is a majority," Thomas Jefferson said.

Another type of political courage is remaining loyal to friends, family, or colleagues who become unpopular. Harry Truman refused to denounce the corrupt Kansas political machine that decades earlier had put him on the path to power, even enduring intense criticism for attending the machine boss's funeral.

Truman stunned critics when, as vice president, he attended the funeral of "Boss Tom" Pendergast a few days after being sworn in and, as it turned out, a few weeks before succeeding Franklin Roosevelt to the presidency. Local newspaper accounts reported that Truman was the only elected official there, even though Pendergast had helped to put hundreds in office.

"He was always my friend and I have always been his," a defiant Truman said.

While some might think Truman's courage to stand up for such a friend was misplaced, his feistiness in the face of political costs became a hallmark of his presidency and earned him kudos from historians.

"I Fired Him Because He Wouldn't Respect the Authority of the President"

Few examples of Truman's courage were more impressive than his firing of one of the nation's most popular figures at the time: General Douglas MacArthur. Hollywood even made a movie about it—*Collision Course*, starring Henry Fonda as MacArthur and E. G. Marshall as Truman.

The episode is a teaching lesson for future presidents on many levels. It was a rare instance of a president resisting the military-minded forces who often push the commander in chief around. It is an enduring showcase for the wisdom of maintaining civilian control of the military. And it is an example of the dangerous tensions that arise between the military leaders and the civilian command in an era of limited wars.

At stake in the Truman-MacArthur showdown was the president's policy that a Cold War against communism would eventually wear it down, as ultimately happened in the 1990s. MacArthur was a leader of the hawks of his day who wanted all-out war to defeat China and the Soviet Union.

MacArthur was a formidable political figure, a military hero who was well known and popular for his exploits going back to World War I when he made it his policy to "lead men from the front," refused to wear a gas mask, and became the most decorated officer of that war.

He received two Distinguished Service Crosses, seven Silver Stars, a Distinguished Service Medal, and two Purple Hearts.

In World War II, MacArthur was Supreme Allied Commander of the Southwest Pacific and gained more fame as the man who formally accepted the Japanese surrender aboard the USS *Missouri* in 1945, which officially ended the war. For the next five and a half years he oversaw the occupation of Japan, winning accolades in Washington and around the country for what historians have called one of the most successful rebuilding efforts of a war-torn nation that the world had ever seen.

Then came Korea, which had been divided into two occupation zones as part of an American deal with the Soviet Union. Communist North Korea invaded the western-aligned South Korea in 1950, provoking Truman to seek United Nations authority for a war. He put MacArthur in charge. Although MacArthur's long experience in the region made him the obvious choice, the arrogant general and Truman were not pals.

It did not help their relations that hawks in the Republican Party who wanted to oust the Democratic president and escalate the Korean War were talking up MacArthur, often called America's greatest living general, as a potential candidate for the White House.

Truman's limited approach to the Korean War was unpopular around the country and MacArthur was quite vocal in complaining about the restrictions placed upon him. China's communist government was assisting North Korea, producing angry calls for the United States to respond by invading China.

Americans were riding high after winning World War II and wanted to see an aggressive and successful prosecution of the war against communism in the region. But Truman and his advisers were deeply worried that an escalation would lead to a world war against China and the Soviet Union. Their idea for limited conflicts in proxy countries was new and unsettling to many, but it was the foundation for what became four decades of American policy against communism.

Truman's breaking point with MacArthur came less than a year after the Korean War started. The president was preparing to engage North Korea and China in peace negotiations, hoping to end the conflict for good. MacArthur was against the talks and tried to undermine a potential peace deal, holding firm to his famous dictum, "In war, there is no substitute for victory."

Historian Robert Smith writes in *MacArthur in Korea: The Naked*

Emperor that MacArthur "undertook to sabotage Truman's effort to open peace negotiations with the Chinese. No one not blinded by hero worship could overlook the arrogance and contempt with which MacArthur deliberately flouted Truman's directive."

The president knew that MacArthur was privately complaining to his Republican foes about the peace plans, but kept quiet until the general went too far by going public. The outspoken general even issued an unauthorized press release containing a veiled threat to expand the war into China. Washington was openly debating the "Truman View" versus the "MacArthur View" on the question of wider war, as though they were equals.

At one o'clock on the morning of April 11, 1951, the White House press team had switchboard operators summon reporters for an emergency press conference. Some of the journalists speculated that Truman, who had lost public support for his limited war policy, was going to cave to MacArthur's stance and call for a declaration of war against China. They were wrong.

The president did not appear at the briefing. Instead, his press secretary handed out a terse statement. It announced that "effective at once" MacArthur was relieved of all his commands because "General of the Army Douglas MacArthur is unable to give his wholehearted support to the policies of the United States and the United Nations."

Later, Truman elaborated on the decision for reporters in his typically blunt fashion. "I fired him because he wouldn't respect the authority of the President. I didn't fire him because he was a dumb son of a bitch, although he was, but that's not against the law for generals. If it was, half to three-quarters of them would be in jail."

Truman suffered a huge political hit for his decision. Although many Americans agreed that MacArthur's insubordination justified the firing, it sparked a roaring debate over the president's refusal to take the fight to communist China. A *Time* magazine editorial predicted that Truman's act "almost certainly brings World War III closer because it throws away a large part of U.S. strength." A congressional investigation of the firing concluded that MacArthur's firing was a "shock to the national pride" and Truman's reasons for it were "utterly inadequate to justify the act."

The political fallout contributed to Truman's eventual decision not to run for reelection the next year. He gets credit for courage in the MacArthur firing and many other decisions, but historians say his political problem was an inability to persuade voters. "He made all the necessary decisions with great and simple courage," Arthur Schlesinger and Richard H. Rovere wrote in *General MacArthur and President Truman: The Struggle for Control of American Foreign Policy,* "but he lacked the gift of illuminating them so that the people as a whole could understand their necessity."

Truman never wavered in defending the correctness of his decision to avoid widening the war against communism by firing MacArthur. History proved him right. It took a long time, but Truman believed that all-out war against communism was unnecessary because one day it would collapse from within. His preference for a Cold War with limited conflicts bore fruit when the Soviet Union finally fell apart and China began to embrace capitalism.

Historians Rovere and Schlesinger write that MacArthur simply did not understand what Truman knew, that communism would be defeated if we took the time to "build an ever-widening circle of allies and friendly neutrals" and wait for "discontent to ferment within the sphere of Soviet power." In other words, as Truman said, MacArthur was a "dumb son of a bitch."

MacArthur returned to Washington after the firing and decided against going into politics. His last public appearance was his famous farewell address to Congress, where he said, "Old soldiers never die; they just fade away. . . . And like the old soldier of that ballad, I now close my military career and just fade away—an old soldier who tried to do his duty as God gave him the light to see that duty. Good-bye."

Truman's firing of "the greatest living general" was a supreme example of political courage.

"No Calls, Got It?"

There are also acts of personal courage, often performed for political reasons, but still acts of bravery in the face of risk. George W.

Bush flew into the war zone in Iraq at a time when the military was fearful to let him do so. Sure, it was done for the uplifting photo opportunity showing the president serving Thanksgiving turkey to the troops, but it was still somewhat of a personal risk.

To reduce the risk, which also served to highlight how dangerous Iraq still was, there was nearly unprecedented secrecy about the president's holiday trip. His parents, the former president and First Lady, were not even told as they arrived at their son's Texas ranch, where they were expecting to spend Thanksgiving with him.

The White House press pool, a rotating contingent of reporters who are usually kept abreast of the president's whereabouts, were also kept in the dark. The pool had already been given a menu of what the family would be having for dinner.

But the truth was that the night before, Bush and National Security Adviser Condoleezza Rice had been driven in an unmarked car with tinted windows from the president's ranch, passing Secret Service agents who were not told what was happening. Both Rice and Bush wore baseball caps, pulled low over their eyes.

The president's family and the news media chosen to join the president were told at the last minute. "I had been taking a nap and had just a few minutes to grab what I need and be outside the back of my hotel and not to make any calls," Agence France-Presse photographer Tim Sloan later told colleagues.

On Air Force One heading for Iraq, Bush admonished the pool of five journalists on board not to break telephone silence. "No calls, got it?" he said, slashing his hand in front of his throat to stress the point.

Air Force One landed in Baghdad in the dark with its lights dimmed. Passengers were told that they could not open their window blinds and risk having the plane detected.

"We want no light emanating from the plane," a press aide explained.

Upon landing, the president ducked into a jeep, accompanied by a motorcade of twelve other vehicles, including a military ambulance. Five minutes later he was inside a military dining facility where more than six hundred surprised troops greeted him.

The world did not learn of Bush's trip until Air Force One was safely returning home.

"He's Not Coming Down Here to Hide"

Perhaps our most tragic example of personal courage in a president was that fateful day in Dallas when John F. Kennedy stepped into an open convertible limousine for a motorcade through a city known to be populated with right-wing radicals who hated him. That was too much courage, Mr. President—remember that!

For good reason, we have not since seen presidents in open cars making themselves targets. There is much dispute and conspiratorial suspicion about the circumstances that led to Kennedy's car being opened as it was on November 22, 1963, devoid of the clear plastic bubble top that, although not bulletproof, might have prevented fatal injuries.

Some say that Kennedy personally made the choice. The Warren Commission, which investigated the assassination shortly afterward, quotes the recollection of a security official who claims that before the Dallas trip one of the president's closest aides, Kenneth O'Donnell, had said, "If the weather is clear and it is not raining, have that bubble top off."

Decades later a special investigative committee of the U.S. House of Representatives reexamined the Kennedy assassination, reporting in 1979 that an aide to Vice President Johnson who coordinated Kennedy's Dallas trip also instructed the removal of the bubble top. That aide was Bill Moyers, who went on to became a well-known broadcast journalist. The House committee cited testimony quoting Moyers telling his Dallas representative to "get that goddamned bubble off unless it's pouring rain."

Moyers told the committee that his only "major decision" was one that happened to underscore the political imperative of the trip: for the president to show the citizens of a politically hostile region that he was not afraid of them.

"There was a dispute as to whether or not to print in the newspapers the [motorcade] route," Moyers told the House committee. "I said, 'Oh, yes they are. He's not coming down here to hide. He's coming down here to get a public reaction, and the decision is to print the route of the President's procession.'"

The absence of Secret Service agents standing near the president on the limousine running boards was also a factor in his death—and another choice attributed to Kennedy himself. The Warren Commission reported that "the President had frequently stated that he did not want agents to ride on these steps during a motorcade except when necessary. He had repeated this wish only a few days before, during his visit to Tampa, Fla."

Flanking motorcycles that could have provided some protection were also ordered away in order to make the president seem more accessible to his public, according to the Warren Commission. "On previous occasions, the President had requested that, to the extent possible, these flanking motorcycles keep back from the sides of his car."

While it is debatable whether different choices about how to handle the motorcade would have made any difference in the assassination of the young president, it is clear that Kennedy himself wanted to openly parade through the streets of Dallas.

The considerations and compromises behind Kennedy's fatal trip reveal a president who, for deeply political reasons, chose to place himself at personal risk.

The internal White House debates about this trip centered on an ideological struggle within the president's Democratic Party. The conservative wing of the party in Texas was led by Governor John B. Connally. Liberals followed Senator Ralph Yarborough.

The 1979 House investigative committee concluded that "in the end, ironically, it was the tension and compromise between the two views that produced the fatal motorcade route. If either side had been able to dictate its desires without compromise, the assassination might never have occurred."

Governor Connally wanted Kennedy to use the trip to strengthen his support among Texas conservatives in the year before the president's reelection campaign. For a venue, he selected the Dallas Trade

Mart, a new convention hall that was the pride of the conservative business community. Its drawback, in the eyes of the more populist-oriented liberal politicians, was the limited number of guests who could be accommodated, making the visit too much about the president stroking conservative elites.

Kennedy believed that his frequent exposure to the people by motorcade was a major factor in his successful campaign for the presidency. He and his aides opposed confining his visit to a private speaking engagement before a select group at the Trade Mart.

Governor Connally objected to a downtown motorcade, fearing the likelihood of embarrassing pickets or unflattering signs. The Texas Democratic Party's executive secretary, Frank Erwin, even went so far as to express to the White House a fear of an embarrassing incident provoked by the state's vigorous right-wing elements.

Radical Texas conservatives had publicly assaulted national Democrats such as Adlai Stevenson in the past, Erwin noted. Connally and his associates were deeply worried about something happening on the motorcade that would tarnish the image of Dallas, although none actually imagined an assassination in the offing.

"Kennedy's wishes prevailed," the House investigative committee reported. "There was a motorcade," although he compromised by agreeing to the Trade Mart event even though liberal Texans and many of his own staff preferred the Women's Building at the city fairgrounds.

For security reasons, the Secret Service also preferred the Women's Building because they could design a motorcade route from there that avoided slow-speed turns—like the one that ended up making Kennedy such an easy target at the infamous Dealey Plaza.

Had either side of this debate prevailed without compromise, Kennedy might have lived.

Listen to Your Security People, Mr. President

The lesson, Mr. President, is that there will be many temptations to risk your life for a political purpose—and there will be times when you must choose to do so. Those charged with protecting your life would prefer keeping you almost completely out of public view, but that is not politically feasible.

But rethink—and rethink again—any decision you make that goes against what your security team recommends. Personal courage can come at great personal cost.

A popular president like Kennedy, who relies on personal charisma before large crowds for political power, faces the greatest danger. Barack Obama is also such a person. His ability to draw massive crowds is unprecedented.

"They Let Me Walk on the Way Back"

Like most presidents, Obama sometimes chafes at the tight security, but handles it with humor. In an appearance on NBC's *The Tonight Show*, President Obama joked about his negotiations with the Secret Service earlier that day over his desire to walk from his helicopter to a rally.

"We landed at the fairground down in Costa Mesa. And I see the fairground where I think we're having this town hall and I said, well, why don't we walk over there? Secret Service says, no, sir, it's seven hundred fifty yards. [Laughter.]

"So I was trying to calculate, well, that's like a five-minute walk? 'Yes, sir. Sorry.' [Laughter.]

"Now, they let me walk on the way back. But, you know, the doctor is behind me with the defibrillator. [Laughter.]"

The dangers to Obama are exacerbated by the hatred that could fester among those who despise his African and Muslim heritage. Too much personal courage in his case is not advisable. His fans should be willing to forgo the massive outdoor gatherings to protect him—or at least be patient with the extensive security that must surround him.

Gone are the days when presidents like Andrew Jackson or Teddy Roosevelt came to power on the strength of legendary tales about great courage in battle as military leaders. And yet a certain expectation remains that our presidents should be brave and strong.

Political courage is the hardest of all. So many of our presidents backed down when faced with tough political choices. Even those who stepped up to the plate on a big issue at other times showed weakness. And often they regretted it.

For all of the credit that Johnson deserves for bucking the political conventions of his day to correct the nation's terrible record on civil rights, he simply caved to the powerful forces who wanted to escalate the Vietnam War.

Johnson privately told White House reporters that he felt trapped into the war. He fretted about being seen as the first president to lose a war, which drove him to allow military planners to keep upping the ante even when his instincts were to pull out.

Lacking the courage to end an unpopular and unsuccessful war destroyed Johnson's presidency, forcing him to back down from running for reelection in 1968. Yet Johnson had the skill to overcome the military, industrial, and political interests clamoring to stay in Vietnam. He just didn't use it.

"If I've Lost Cronkite, I've Lost Middle America"

If only Johnson had ended the Vietnam War by mustering the same masterful abilities he had deployed so effectively on civil rights, he would not have left such a scar on his presidency.

Johnson later complained that he had listened too much to the generals who told him what they thought he wanted to hear: the good news. But the press corps could hear his doubts in those off-the-record sessions. He knew that a change was needed. He just could not call up the courage to pull out of Vietnam.

Instead, Johnson pulled out of the presidency itself. When the early voting in the Democratic nomination race of 1968 showed his weakness within his own party, Johnson had to recognize that he had lost the people.

The final straw came when CBS news anchor Walter Cronkite

reported on a trip to Vietnam and announced that the nation was losing the war. "If I've lost Cronkite, I've lost middle America," Johnson told aides.

When Cronkite, who had earned his war reporting credentials as a correspondent during World War II and Korea, delivered his fateful broadcast on February 27, 1968, U.S. forces had just been surprised and overwhelmed by the Tet Offensive. North Vietnamese troops had invaded the soil of our ally, South Vietnam, and for a time even seized the U.S. embassy in the capital of Saigon.

Meanwhile antiwar sentiments back home were peaking.

Publicly, Johnson thought he was displaying courage by maintaining the course in a difficult war. But it was really political cowardice that directed him. Powerful leaders in the Congress and at the Pentagon had pushed the president to keep going.

We do not have to imagine the angst and regret as Johnson watched Cronkite's live broadcast that night. He openly expressed it and, little more than a month later, essentially gave up his presidency, announcing that he would not seek reelection.

By today's standards, Cronkite's words might not seem so provocative. But in the couched terms for objective journalists of his day it was a stunning rebuke of the president's policies:

> We have been too often disappointed by the optimism of the American leaders, both in Vietnam and Washington, to have faith any longer in the silver linings they find in the darkest clouds. . . . For it seems now more certain than ever that the bloody experience of Vietnam is to end in a stalemate. . . . It is increasingly clear to this reporter that the only rational way out then will be to negotiate, not as victors, but as an honorable people who lived up to their pledge to defend democracy, and did the best they could.
>
> This is Walter Cronkite. Good night.

What is so ironic about Cronkite's words is that Johnson seemed to privately agree, but could not gather the courage to tell the American people the hard truth and to lead the country out of the war.

Instead, just thirty-three days after Cronkite lowered the boom, Johnson broadcast a very different speech from the Oval Office:

> With America's sons in the fields far away, with America's future under challenge right here at home, with our hopes and the world's hopes for peace in the balance every day, I do not believe that I should devote an hour or a day of my time to any personal partisan causes or to any duties other than the awesome duties of this office—the Presidency of your country. Accordingly, I shall not seek, and I will not accept, the nomination of my party for another term as your President.

In a way it was courageous for Johnson to step down. Politics was his lifeblood. Giving up his great love for being president was unimaginably painful for him, but he knew the country had gotten away from him and, for its sake, he had to walk away.

Although many in the press room empathized with his plight, there were jokes about the poor foreman back at Johnson's Texas ranch. For everyone knew that this restless man who loved control would be ordering around his ranch hands with the same zeal that he had shown in running the country.

As contrast to Johnson's lack of political courage undermining his presidency and his legacy, other chief executives lost power because of their courage—although in some cases their legacies later thrived because of it.

Giving Away the Panama Canal

Jimmy Carter gave away the Panama Canal, provoking histrionic protests from conservatives. Actor John Wayne led a public relations campaign to keep the canal as U.S.-owned territory, but Carter used a sizable fortune in political chits to force the move through Congress.

A long line of Carter's predecessors in the White House had

known that the U.S. occupation of the canal zone was a bone of contention in Southern Hemisphere relations that needed to be removed. No one before him had the courage to do it, fearing the image of weakness it would create at home. The political costs just did not seem worth it.

Since its construction at the urging of Teddy Roosevelt, this conduit of international maritime trade was a great symbol of national ingenuity and skill for many prideful Americans. But to Central and South American nations the Panama Canal was a hated symbol of our arrogance, a constant source of complications for our relations and trade with the region.

Carter's proposal to cede the canal to Panama's government produced the very political backlash that earlier presidents had feared. Senate conservatives such as Strom Thurmond (R-S.C.) and Jesse Helms (R-N.C.) mounted full-scale political offensives against it, arguing that it would be the surrender of a strategic American asset to what they considered to be a hostile government.

Thurmond put it quite bluntly during the debates over Carter's treaty, saying, "The canal is ours, we bought and we paid for it and we should keep it."

Carter's politically courageous step to remove this thorn in U.S. relations with the Southern Hemisphere was certainly no panacea. Years later, President George H. W. Bush invaded Panama to remove and arrest its criminal despot, dictator Manuel Noriega.

In the long run it has been helpful to U.S. interests that Carter took this action. Decades of riots and political demagoguery against the U.S. occupation of the canal zone were stopped.

Still, it was not helpful to Carter's political future, as it became a cause célèbre for his victorious opponent, Republican Ronald Reagan, in the 1980 presidential election.

"We Begin Bombing in Five Minutes"

Reagan found a more politically palatable way to show political courage during his tenure. He challenged the Soviet Union with budget-busting defense spending at a time when many Americans saw anticommunism as a quaint relic of the 1950s. Although the demise of our Cold War foe came after his presidency, Reagan's obsession with the Soviet Union is widely credited for breaking up the communist empire.

The political downside of Reagan's defense spending to intimidate the Soviets was the resulting deficits and an overall national debt larger than all previous debt accumulated by all of his predecessors combined. That alone could have become a huge political risk for a less skilled president.

Reagan's reflexive anticommunism became a vehicle for political opponents who tried to label him a warmonger. He lent support to these charges with an ill-advised joke during a microphone check before a national broadcast. Thinking there was no recording under way, Reagan said, "My fellow Americans, I'm pleased to tell you today that I've signed legislation that will outlaw Russia forever. We begin bombing in five minutes."

Of course, for Reagan's conservative base, there was no political risk in saber rattling against communists with boosts in defense spending (even if it did come at the cost of rising deficits that alarmed fiscal conservatives). But then, late in his presidency, Reagan engineered a reversal of engines that had his conservative friends reeling. He reached out to Mikhail Gorbachev.

Correctly perceiving weakness among the Soviets, the Reagan White House made overtures. Reagan himself took it even further than his own aides when at a meeting with Gorbachev he stunned the Soviet leader by proposing that both nations abolish nuclear weapons.

Suddenly, Reagan's conservative allies were griping that he was a peacenik who did not understand the Soviet menace.

Historian Michael Beschloss, in his book *Presidential Courage*, cites Reagan's outreach to Gorbachev among his nine examples of bravery in the White House going all the way back to George Washington.

"Ronald Reagan made a lot of risky decisions to end the Cold War," Beschloss said in a 2007 interview on PBS television. "He said

Mikhail Gorbachev is for real, I think we can really do this, abolish nuclear weapons. The people who were most angry at him were most of his oldest supporters who loved him when he was a Cold Warrior. The point is that Reagan understood that, you know, we always hear about a politician holding on to his or her political base. Reagan knew that, yes, hold on to your base, but in the end, you have to be its leader and not its captive."

Regardless of whether one sees courage in Reagan's policies regarding the Soviets, Beschloss provides an excellent definition of a significant variation on political courage: standing up to your base.

"Be the Leader of Your Political Base, Mr. President, Not Its Captive"

Bill Clinton learned the peril of feeding the base early in his presidency. It was a courageous effort, but then fear set in and Clinton moved to the ideological center for his reelection campaign.

Democrats were full of themselves as Clinton took office in 1993. They had been out of the White House for twelve years.

Clinton quickly indulged his party's liberal base on issues ranging from gun control and gays in the military to universal health insurance. But his early courage soon disappeared as conservatives successfully fought back and defeated much of his agenda.

The GOP took control of Congress during the midterm election of 1994 largely on the strength of blasting Clinton's liberal initiatives. The Democrats were on the run. To make things worse, Clinton joined with Republicans—infuriating his liberal base—to enact welfare reforms that cut programs for the poor. Even some on the president's own staff were enraged by this move. His lack of courage in sticking to his original ideals might have helped Clinton win reelection in 1996, but it reduced his effectiveness as president.

In the end, the Clinton presidency is destined to be remembered most for beating the impeachment rap in a Senate trial over his sex life. That sordid affair and his abandonment of Democratic Party principles on the big issues robbed the promise of a president who had the wit and skill to be great.

From either side of the ideological fence, it might be good politics to move to the center, Mr. President. But it is not courageous.

Democrat Barack Obama tries a little of both—moving toward the political center on some things, while at other times delivering what liberals on Capitol Hill want.

Some partisan Democrats grumbled, for instance, when he chose to keep the outgoing president's Republican defense secretary and initially balked at doing away with George W. Bush's tax cuts for the wealthy. But liberals in Congress were pleased when Obama backed massive spending on infrastructure and social programs to stimulate the economy.

Still, Obama is mindful of the dangers of letting liberals give ammunition to conservatives, who look for every opportunity to label him a "socialist" who wants "to spread the wealth around."

Obama's courage in opposing the war in Iraq from the start faced hard tests once he took office, especially when unequivocal calls to end the war devolved into ever-lengthening timetables that were essentially what the Bush administration had established. This deference to the military, industrial, and political establishment's desire to maintain a war footing in the Middle East is very reminiscent of Johnson's failure to challenge the same forces over the Vietnam War—a decision Johnson came to regret until his dying day.

Obama risks repeating Johnson's mistakes by listening too much to the generals. Obama ordered more troops into Afghanistan on the generals' promise that escalation will lead to victory. Unfortunately, that's what the British and the Russians thought before they utterly failed to subdue their foes in Afghanistan's difficult terrain.

You Are the Decision Maker, Not the Follower

Have courage to resist such pleas if your instincts say otherwise, Mr. President. That is why the founders of our nation put a civil servant in charge of the military. You are the decision maker, not the follower.

It is easier to talk tough when on the outside looking in. Once you are president, however, the pressure is on. Presidents too often yield to those pressing for excessive military and intelligence tools out of fear that they will be seen as weaklings. Presidents who rise from the liberal side of our political spectrum are even more vulnerable to such arguments. The military establishment and their friends in Congress are quick to exploit any sign that a new Democratic president is not strong on defense, saying he lacks courage to protect the nation.

In what appears to be an endless war against terrorism, the bullying of presidents can only get worse. The real courage is in standing firm against such pressure, Mr. President. Learn from your predecessors who lost so much when they privately submitted in order to publicly appear courageous.

Give the citizens your courage as you take office, Mr. President, not after you leave. Some of their bravest speeches were not given until the presidents were leaving office, or later.

Parting Shots

Every new president ought to go back and read some of what his predecessors said as they left office. It is during these moments when they are free of political concerns and the grip of powerful interests that limited their actions, these are the moments when presidents tell us what they really think.

How wonderful it would be to take these lessons to heart on your own Inauguration Day, Mr. President, instead of waiting until the final days before your successor takes over.

In the last days of his presidency, Dwight D. Eisenhower cautioned that the "federal government's collaboration with an alliance of military and industrial leaders, though necessary, was vulnerable to abuse of power."

Eisenhower also warned that American citizens need "to be vigilant in monitoring the military-industrial complex. Only an alert and knowledgeable citizenry can compel the proper meshing of the huge industrial and military machinery of defense with all peaceful methods and goals, so that security and liberty may prosper together."

Other presidents also had something to say in their parting shots.

President Lyndon B. Johnson said, "Every president lives, not only with what is, but with what has been and what could be."

As he left the White House, Jimmy Carter said the "presidency is the most powerful office in the world and among the most severely constrained by law and custom." He also said, "Thoughtful criticism and close scrutiny of all government officials by the press and the public are an important part of a democratic society."

Ronald Reagan took his leave from the White House with "a final word for the men and women of the Reagan revolution, the men and women across America, who for eight years did the work that brought America back. My friends, we did it. We weren't just marking time. We made a difference."

Mr. President, whatever you do in office, have the courage to make a difference.

SEVEN

GIVE US VISION:
IT'S YOUR LEGACY

*First of all, let me assert my firm belief that the only thing we have
to fear is fear itself—nameless, unreasoning, unjustified terror which
paralyzes needed efforts to convert retreat into advance.*
—FRANKLIN D. ROOSEVELT

When it comes to laying out a vision, some presidents get it and some don't.

Get it, Mr. President. Your job is not only a to-do list for making appointments, passing laws, and negotiating treaties. To succeed you must also inspire us to the future—with words and deeds.

A good president, wrote nineteenth-century historian Henry Adams, "resembles the commander of a ship at sea. He must have a helm to grasp, a course to steer, a port to seek."

The port you seek, Mr. President, is your vision. Those who take this lightly do so at their peril.

George H. W. Bush clearly did not get it in 1987 as he prepared to run for the presidency.

Bush benefited from the popularity of the man he had served as vice president for two terms. If anything, Ronald Reagan was all about vision. "Less government and more freedom was his mantra."

Lofty words and thoughts did not come easily to Bush. Ideas and ideologies did not move him. Essentially, he was a lifelong bureaucrat more stirred by practical evaluations of tangible problems followed by pragmatic solutions.

"A man of action rather than reflection" was how *Time* magazine described Bush in a profile coinciding with the launch of his campaign. Whenever asked what he would do as president, Bush typically responded that he would pick the best people and run an efficient government.

Bush's lack of interest in the big-picture rhetoric worried friends and advisers as he gathered steam for a White House run. To many, his idea of an argument for his candidacy could be summed up in three words: It's my turn.

After all, as a dutiful vice president, he had attended all the meetings he was called to, seldom took notes that could get him or anyone else in trouble, and rarely asked a question or tipped his hand in a way that proved whose side he was on in a difficult debate.

This ultimate bureaucrat had a problem, however—one that dogged him throughout the campaign and into his presidency. Conservative columnist George Will bluntly described Bush's limitation in those days: "He does not say why he wants to be there, so the public does not know why it should care if he gets his way."

"Oh, the Vision Thing"

Bush himself gave his critics the words that came to symbolize his lack of appreciation for a president's overarching purpose in our politics. The story got out early in the 1988 campaign about a session with advisers when he asked for a list of expected issues in the upcoming race.

Instead of the to-do list he asked for, the vice president was given an earful about his need to inspire voters. He should go to Camp David, the advisers said, and think about where he wanted to take the country.

"Oh, the vision thing," Bush said.

To Bush, the "vision thing" was just another item on the checklist, something you could always hire speechwriters to craft. He never did internalize a clarity of ideas and principles that could shape public opinion and influence Congress. It could be the biggest reason that Bush lost reelection four years later.

Bush could not live down his "vision thing" comment. No matter how hard he tried to demonstrate his hopes and dreams for the nation, it always seemed phony and awkward because most observers believed that his originally dismissive attitude of the concept reflected his true self.

In the presidential game, there is no vision without the right words. Indeed, it is your words that convey your vision, Mr. President.

That is why accomplished speechwriters have become a fixture at the White House, although they are expected to stay behind the scenes. Although it is an open secret that presidents generally read aloud words written for them, they naturally prefer that everyone pretend otherwise. Aides often go to great lengths to stress how much input the boss gave, but it can be difficult to pin them down on the details of which words the president actually wrote.

A standard line is that the speechwriters meet in advance with the president and receive his wisdom about what should be included as if he were some sort of oracle and they are merely the stenographers. Not likely.

If the speech turns out to be a great one, ambitious speechwriters find a way to leak the truth of their authorship. Particularly successful words or phrases from presidential speeches become trademarks for the once anonymous authors. Some even come to be identified by these words for the rest of their careers. Occasionally, disputes arise between former speechwriters about who actually authored a famous phrase.

Of course, if the speech is a flop, the writers are only too happy to continue giving the president all the credit.

Beware of this little game, Mr. President. If you have not yet learned how to write some nifty language for a speech, get started. Otherwise, credit for some of your best moments will one day be given to someone else. And if you do craft some powerful words, make sure there is proof that you wrote them.

Elements of a Good Presidential Speech

The elements of successful presidential addresses are fairly basic, but take different forms. Sometimes there is an identifiable foe to denounce. The more identifiable, the easier it will be to nail the speech.

Barack Obama was in a sense lucky that the nation was gripped by hard economic times when he took office. When Americans are squeezing their wallets, they are most likely to pay attention to the president.

Or, as the saying goes in politics, the best way to reach the voters' hearts is through their wallets.

Whatever the dilemma of the day might be, a good presidential speech needs to stick to a central theme. This is your vision, Mr. President. Give it plenty of thought, even if others write the actual words.

Often, presidential speeches are written by committee, and you can tell. They ramble from one theme to the next. State of the Union addresses are particularly susceptible to this, as members of Congress lobby the White House to include their pet themes or projects. The result is that most State of the Union addresses become a mishmash, a laundry list of proposals that lack a greater theme.

A few memorable phrases are essential. Again, dramatic events make that easier. Who can forget Franklin Roosevelt's words to Congress urging war against Japan: "Yesterday, December 7, 1941—a date which will live in infamy—the United States was suddenly and deliberately attacked by the naval and air forces of the Japanese empire. . . ."

Modern presidential speechwriters do their best to keep the beginning and end as cohesive and thematic as possible, knowing that any number of items will be inserted by the various aides and officials (including the president). Writers try to stuff those things in the middle, jealously protecting the opening and closing remarks.

Presidents differ in how they interact with their writers. Clinton, himself a decent writer, loved to fiddle with wording all the way through to the final draft. For one State of the Union address he was still rewriting in the limousine on the way to Capitol Hill, causing confusion among staff aides charged with installing the speech in the machinery for his TelePrompTer. As a result, the wrong text appeared on the screen as Clinton spoke.

Thanks, however, to Clinton's personal involvement in the drafting, he knew the wording well enough to wing it until the correct text appeared. No one knew anything was wrong.

Some presidents would rely on an ultimate authority figure who could change the final language. Harry Truman turned over the final versions of speeches to his wife, Bess. His speechwriters claimed that she nearly always added a human touch that improved the wording.

Nixon sought ideological balance among his speechwriters, including conservatives, moderates, and, for him, somewhat left-leaning wordsmiths.

Eisenhower was unusual in that he had actually been a speechwriter during his military service—he crafted words for General MacArthur. As a result of this background, Eisenhower was known for putting his writers through as many as a dozen drafts for a single speech.

Calvin Coolidge hired the first professional speechwriter in the White House, and they have been there ever since. Coolidge's wordsmith was a Republican politician named Judson Welliver. Today, a society of speechwriters in Washington is named after him.

It would be nice if presidents took more time to hone their thoughts and vision into words. They could probably deliver them more effectively, giving the language a more authentic sound. But the usual response to such a suggestion is the president does not have time.

Make time, Mr. President. Do not let words be put into your mouth on every occasion. When setting forth your vision for the country's future it is especially vital that you at least put some of the words together.

There was a time, believe it or not, when presidents actually wrote their own speeches. Most political figures did so during the eighteenth and nineteenth centuries when strong oratory was the principal skill required to be elected. Being able to speak in public for hours with few notes was a prerequisite for office.

George Washington was an exception. He rose to fame as a general and not as a career politician, so he was unskilled in the speech arts. Alexander Hamilton sometimes helped Washington with his speechwriting. Historians believe that Hamilton was the principal author of Washington's famous farewell address.

Abraham Lincoln was probably one of the best speechwriters ever to serve in the White House. If for nothing else, the Gettysburg Address earned him that title.

A Heap of Vision in Ten Sentences

What is so remarkable about the Gettysburg Address is that in just a two-minute speech Lincoln set forth one of the great visions in presidential history. Drawing upon the principles of human equality in the Declaration of Independence, he redefined the ongoing Civil War not so much as a struggle to preserve the Union but as a "new birth of freedom" with true equality of all citizens as its goal. He also ensured in this speech that winning the war would elevate the status of national government over states' rights.

That is a heap of vision for ten sentences and two hundred seventy-two words. And yet there was no bevy of professional writers swirling around Lincoln as he wrote what became one of the most quoted speeches in history.

A popular myth is that Lincoln wrote the Gettysburg Address on the back of an envelope while riding the train to the speech site. That has never been confirmed and seems most unlikely. Lincoln crafted his speeches with great care. He often wrote several drafts. Many of his handwritten drafts for the Gettysburg Address later surfaced, and none of them were on the back of an envelope. Like most of his speeches, they were written on Executive Mansion stationery.

Lincoln actually wrote the first drafts in Washington. And eyewitnesses said he completed the final draft in the home of the Gettysburg lawyer where he spent the night before giving the speech.

Also, the political significance of what Lincoln was attempting to do in this address suggests that he would not have been so cavalier as to dash it off on any available piece of paper while riding the train. In his view, the preservation of the union was not the only thing at stake. The preservation of his own presidency was in doubt.

By late 1863, when he traveled to Gettysburg, Pennsylvania, to deliver the address, the casualty list from the bloody war was rising at an alarming rate. At least a quarter of a million lives had been lost. Antiwar sentiment was raging throughout the Northern states and Lincoln was its target. Democrats were eager to oust Lincoln, the first Republican president, in the next election, just a year away. They proposed ending the war by making concessions to the South.

Lincoln's predicament was made worse by the necessity of a draft to keep the ravaged Union battle lines supplied with fresh troops. Antidraft riots were breaking out. Hatred of the president was rampant. Just two months before the Gettysburg Address the governor of Pennsylvania and a close friend, Andrew Curtin, wrote an ominous letter to Lincoln, warning the president that the public was turning against him and the war:

> I have been looking over the canvass in this State, with great care, and have formed the following conclusions: If the election were to occur now, the result would be extremely doubtful, and although most of our discreet friends are sanguine of the result, my impression is, the chances would be against us. The draft is very odious in the State, and unfortunately is not producing more than one-sixth of the men anticipated for the public service. In the cities and towns the changes are all in our favor, but in the country, remote from the centres of intelligence, the Democratic leaders have succeeded in exciting prejudice and passion, and have infused their poison into the minds of the people to a very large extent, and the changes are against us.... It is impossible to magnify the importance of the result of the election in this State to the Country, and I desire to sink all personal consid-

erations, and all political and personal differences and dis-
agreements, and give the Contest all my time and energies.

Those are not words any president wants to hear just a year
before facing reelection. Lincoln had to give the country a brand-
new vision for the war that would raise spirits and reset the resolve
to press on.

It is fascinating that, in choosing a venue to proclaim his vision to
keep the war going, Lincoln selected a battlefield where some eight
thousand soldiers and several thousand horses had perished. If anything, Gettysburg was a reminder of his war's tremendous cost. But
how wise it turned out to be.

In the speech, Lincoln appealed for going forward to victory or
else the dead would have lost their lives "in vain." The horrifying
drama of the scene at Gettysburg intensified the impact of his words.

Critics to this day have pointed out that the Gettysburg Address
was long on poetry and short on logic. Would democracy throughout
the world have perished if the Confederacy had survived? It seems a
stretch for Lincoln to have asserted that the Union must fight the war
to a successful conclusion so that "government of the people, by the
people, for the people, should not perish from the earth."

Journalist H. L. Mencken wrote in 1922 that "it is difficult to
imagine anything more untrue" than Lincoln's claim that the war
was being fought to preserve democracy. "The Union soldiers in the
battle actually fought against self-determination; it was the Confed-
erates who fought for the right of their people to govern themselves,"
Mencken wrote.

Such naysaying aside, there is no question that Lincoln's gambit
worked. His larger vision for the war's purpose eventually rallied the
nation to the great cause he had set forth—the defense of freedom.

Sound familiar? Presidents who run wars usually echo Lincoln's
words, whether it be Reagan's support of the Nicaraguan "freedom
fighters" or George W. Bush's crusade for democracy in the Middle
East. There is no better compliment for a president's vision than to
have it last through the ages as a useful tool for successors, whether
or not it is appropriate.

Presidents in less dramatic times still must find their vision, but it is difficult. In a moment of crisis or when at war, the nation is almost conditioned to rally around a president's vision.

Vision Others Don't See

In peacetime presidents usually must persuade the nation that a cause is worth rallying around, which can be a most difficult task even if it should be done. Defining a vision that Americans are not ready to see takes a great deal of skill.

Jimmy Carter, a trained engineer, tried to inspire the nation to conserve energy. He was right, of course. Had the country listened to him, we might not be so reliant on the foreign oil that sometimes strangles us and keeps us so involved in events in the Middle East. But Americans seek more from their president than admonitions to use less gas. Many laughed at Carter's obsession. People stayed in their cars even though public buses throughout the nation featured placards bearing the president's signature and proclaiming "Thank you for riding the bus."

Interestingly, another president with an engineering background—Herbert Hoover—failed to understand the expansive role expected of a president. His principal failure as the Great Depression descended upon the nation was in not understanding how much Americans needed uplifting leadership—in other words, a vision for a better future. Then along came Franklin Roosevelt, perhaps the most visionary president of modern times, to replace Hoover's technocratic ways with a symphony of words and deeds that changed the nation forever. Roosevelt set the gold standard for presidential vision with those memorable words from his first Inaugural Address: "The only thing we have to fear is fear itself."

It is not that the line was especially original. Eight decades earlier Henry David Thoreau had written, "Nothing is so much to be feared as fear." Roosevelt's advisers later said the phrase had appeared in a department store newspaper advertisement a month before the address.

The "fear itself" line resonated because, like any well-crafted presidential vision statement, it so perfectly fit the man and his times, and set a course for action.

Vision Requires Action Too

Telling Americans to fight their fear was not just rhetoric. Roosevelt's inauguration on March 4, 1933, came in the middle of a bank panic. Fear of bank closures provoked desperate account holders to storm the banks and withdraw their funds, causing further closures. National leadership was sorely needed to stem the panic.

Roosevelt immediately followed his stirring words with action. On the day after his speech the new president declared a "bank holiday," which, for four days, forced the closing of the nation's banks and halted all financial transactions.

Stopping the frantic run on banks gave Roosevelt time to push the Emergency Banking Act through Congress before the four-day "holiday" had ended. The legislation also cleared the way for solvent banks to resume business as early as March 10. Just three days later, nearly a thousand banks were up and running again. The quick success in halting bank failures set the path for a series of steps in the coming weeks that paused the economy's disastrous downward slide.

Even the most inspirational vision is just talk if not combined with action. By telling citizens to stop fearing their fear, Roosevelt was showing how panic over bank failures was compounding itself and actually causing the failures. But had he not acted so quickly with legislation to fix the banking system, his encouraging words would have rung hollow.

Roosevelt also was the perfect person to recommend against giving in to fear. After contracting polio and losing the use of his legs, he had overcome an emotionally crippling fear of drowning by learning to stand and nearly walk in the buoyant waters at Warm Springs.

It is probably no accident that the rest of Roosevelt's quote refers to how unreasoning fear "paralyzes needed efforts to convert retreat into advance." Here was a paralyzed man who had risen to become our president. There could be no better role model for motivating a nation out of its economic paralysis.

"Predominantly a Place of Moral Leadership"

Years later, toward the end of a presidency that lasted almost four terms, Roosevelt was asked for his thoughts on what it takes to succeed in the White House. "It is not merely an administrative office," he said. "It is more than an engineering job, efficient or inefficient. It is predominantly a place of moral leadership. All our great presidents were leaders of thought at times when certain historic ideas in the life of the nation had to be clarified."

Pulitzer Prize–winning historian Arthur M. Schlesinger Jr. notes that "vision per se is not necessarily a good thing." When visions "harden into dogmatic ideologies," he wrote, "they become inhuman, cruel and dangerous."

The Wrong Vision

George W. Bush seemed all too eager to replace his father's lack of vision with the wrong view of the nation's future. Journalist Bob Woodward, who interviewed the second President Bush for four hours while researching his book *Bush at War,* came away with the conclusion that "the president was casting his mission and that of the country in the grand vision of God's master plan."

This "messianic tinge," as Schlesinger called it, caused Bush to wrongly think that American troops invading Iraq would be hailed as liberators and that Iraqis would eagerly embrace our democratic ideals. To his last days in office, the president believed that his war would eventually produce a domino effect, spreading democracy throughout the Islamic world.

Bush got a jarring challenge to his vision on his last trip to Iraq as president. During his press conference in Baghdad an Iraqi journalist threw his shoes at him. Not that the journalist was in the right—

he certainly was not—but it symbolized how wrong Bush's vision had been. It was not the hero's welcome Bush had imagined when he first chose to invade Iraq.

Hitting someone with a shoe is a deep insult in the Arab world, signifying that the person being struck is as low as the dirt beneath the sole of a shoe. Compounding the insult were the assailant's words as he hurled his footwear: "This is a gift from the Iraqis; this is the farewell kiss, you dog!" Among Arabs, who traditionally consider dogs unclean, those words were a strong condemnation. And the insult resounded throughout Arab communities. Thousands of demonstrators in several countries marched to defend the "shoe assailant."

Just a month earlier the American people had delivered their own insult to Bush's vision. His Republican Party, the GOP, was repudiated at the polls. Once the dust settled on the 2008 election, the Democrats had taken the White House and boosted their majorities in Congress.

Bush was so reviled that the GOP presidential nominee, John McCain, was forced to run away from him, not once asking the president to campaign on his behalf.

Time will tell whether Bush's vision of American-sponsored democracy in the Middle East becomes reality, but during his time in office the U.S. occupation of Iraq produced little more than chaos and death, bringing shame upon Bush in the eyes of his countrymen and around the world.

"Some visions are intelligent and benign," Schlesinger said. "Other visions are stupid and malevolent."

"Steady the Ship"

The Bush presidencies reflect mirror images of bad vision. Bush the elder had no vision, while his son's was flawed.

George W. Bush deserves credit for getting it right shortly after the September 11, 2001, attacks on the World Trade Center and the Pentagon. He did not write the speech that he gave at the National Cathedral, but it was a stellar example of a president capturing the moment and providing the nation with a powerful vision at a time when it was most needed.

Sometimes vision is not just about ably steering the ship of state to distant ports, as Henry Adams described. There are times of stress when the commander must simply steady the ship.

In what *USA Today* heralded as "945 words of sorrow and defiance" and only three days after the shocking loss of life on 9/11, Bush declared the nation in "the middle hour of our grief."

With former presidents, including his father, and other dignitaries sitting before him in the ornate cathedral that sits on some of Washington's highest ground, Bush's firm demeanor and soulful tone of voice matched the eloquence of the words written for him. Gone was the aw-shucks manner that he so often displayed in less somber times. The speech, televised throughout the world, contributed in large part to a boost in opinion polls that put him at the peak of his presidency, hovering at around a 90 percent approval:

> Our country was attacked with deliberate and massive cruelty. We have seen the images of fire and ashes and bent steel. Now come the names, the list of casualties we are only beginning to read. They are the names of men and women who began their day at a desk or in an airport, busy with life. They are the names of people who faced death and in their last moments called home to say, "Be brave," and, "I love you." They are the names of passengers who defied their murderers and prevented the murder of others on the ground. They are the names of men and women who wore the uniform of the United States and died at their posts. They are the names of rescuers, the ones whom death found running up the stairs and into the fires to help others. We will read all these names. We will linger over them and learn their stories, and many Americans will weep. To the children and parents and spouses and families and friends of the lost, we offer the deepest sympathy of the Nation. And I assure you, you are not alone.

Written in part by accomplished wordsmith Michael Gerson, the so-called Cathedral Speech is one of Bush's best. Its power and clarity are likely to resonate for generations to come.

Gerson, who stayed at the Bush White House for several more years, later described the pressure that he and the other speechwriters felt in those dark days. "Sometimes the words really do matter," he said. "I felt that way after September 11, where if we had done a poor job, it would have hurt the country."

At a breakfast meeting with reporters in 2006, Gerson elaborated on the importance of presidential speechmaking in difficult times.

"We felt very consciously that we were in a situation like Truman at the beginning of the Cold War, where you had to put in place new institutions and rally the American people to a long struggle, and explain it," Gerson said. "Because it was different from World War II or other wars. This was the challenge . . . to inspire, inform and prepare people for a different kind of war."

As things turned out, Bush's execution of policy in later years fell short of some of the defiant promises in the Cathedral Speech, but on that day he certainly met the moment that the nation was looking for. "Americans do not have the distance of history," Bush said on September 14, 2001, "but our responsibility to history is already clear: to answer these attacks and rid the world of evil."

Bush added: "This conflict was begun on the timing and terms of others. It will end in a way and at an hour of our choosing."

As Bush left office more than seven years later, the "way and hour of our choosing" had still not come. The nation was still at war in Iraq, fighting in Afghanistan, and still looking for Osama bin Laden, the man who had instigated the 9/11 attacks.

Despite the eloquence of his own vision in those early days, Bush ended up missing the mark.

Consoler in Chief

Consoling the nation in times of need has become a presidential trademark. Bill Clinton met such a moment after the horrific 1995 bombing of a federal building in Oklahoma City, costing one hundred sixty-eight lives and injuring eight hundred people.

The assailants, part of a domestic militia movement, had filled a rental truck with more than six thousand pounds of ammonium nitrate fertilizer, nitromethane, Tovex, and diesel fuel. The bomb was detonated in front of the nine-story Alfred P. Murrah Federal Building. Its blast destroyed a third of the building and created a thirty-foot-wide, eight-foot-deep crater. More than three hundred buildings in a sixteen-block radius were severely damaged. More than eighty cars were destroyed or burned. Shattering glass from area buildings accounted for some five percent of the death toll and most of the injuries.

Clinton's much-praised appearance at a memorial service in Oklahoma City eased the nation's shock and ended up being an important political turning point for him. For Americans who felt such deep sympathy for those directly affected, the televised scenes of the president embracing the distraught families of victims made him something of a surrogate consoler for the entire nation.

And once again, a president's words at a memorial service met the moment.

> This terrible sin took the lives of our American family, innocent children in that building only because their parents were trying to be good parents as well as good workers, citizens in the building going about their daily business and many there who served the rest of us, who worked to help the elderly and the disabled, who worked to support our farmers and our veterans, who worked to enforce our laws and to protect us. Let us say clearly, they served us well, and we are grateful. But for so many of you they were also neighbors and friends. You saw them at church or the PTA meetings, at the civic clubs, at the ball park. You know them in ways that all the rest of America could not. And to all the members of the families here present who have suffered loss, though we share your grief, your pain is unimaginable, and we know that. We cannot undo it. That is God's work.

While the genuineness of Clinton's efforts should not be discounted, it also served as a political boost when he most needed it. The year before, his Democratic Party had suffered crushing losses at the ballot box, giving Republicans control of Congress. The next year he would face reelection and, because many observers blamed him for his party's defeats, the assumption was that Clinton might have a tough time keeping the presidency.

Clinton's Oklahoma trip began what became a huge political turnaround for the president, who won reelection by a comfortable margin in 1996.

Going to the Moon

Perhaps the loftiest realized vision for any president was John F. Kennedy's call to go to the moon. It was one of this young president's many challenges to Americans to see beyond self, beyond state lines, beyond national borders, and, in this case, even beyond our very planet.

So much of what Kennedy pursued in his short time was about leading the country to think globally. He created the Peace Corps. He signed the first Nuclear Test Ban Treaty.

When calling for a test-ban treaty with the Soviet Union, Kennedy used uplifting words that would have been nothing more than rhetoric had he not followed them with four months of intense negotiations that culminated in the signing of the historic pact.

This was a time when the threat of nuclear war haunted Americans. It was not only the stuff of movies or legend. They had seen the brink of disaster in the Cuban missile crisis. The Cold War was very much on their minds.

Kennedy pointed the way to a different port on June 10, 1963, and put his call for a nuclear treaty in the fullest context imaginable. His goal was simple and stirring: world peace.

"What kind of peace do I mean?" he asked the audience at American University in Washington. "Not the peace of the grave or the security of the slave. I am talking about genuine peace, the kind of peace that makes life on earth worth living, the kind that enables men and nations to grow and to hope and to build a better life for their children—not merely peace for Americans but peace for all men and women—not merely peace in our time but peace for all time."

Now, that is an ambitious vision—to make life worth living through peace, for the whole world. And in his brief one thousand days as president, Kennedy left a legacy of nuclear containment that really did move the world a big step out of the darkness.

In setting course for the moon, Kennedy eyed a very distant port that was yet another angle in his vision to change the world. He issued the challenge to a joint session of Congress in the first year of his presidency: "I believe that this nation should commit itself to achieving the goal, before this decade is out, of landing a man on the moon and returning him safely to the Earth."

Official Washington was not sure how to take this. Some in the circles of power thought it was an impossible dream from a foolishly idealistic poser. Others saw it as a cynically strategic move in the Cold War chess match between the United States and the Soviet Union.

Perhaps there was some reality to the strategic aims. Kennedy had just been humiliated in the Bay of Pigs fiasco in Cuba, a communist ally of Moscow. In the same speech, he did call for many measures to combat communism, requesting billions, for example, to stop insurgencies in Vietnam.

How odd that in a single speech Kennedy put forth two visions that could not have turned out so differently. We made it to the moon in less than ten years, but a decade later we left Vietnam in shame.

Kennedy had appealed to national pride in calling for a moon mission. The Soviets were hammering us in the final frontier. They sent the Sputnik satellite into orbit in 1957. Four years later, cosmonaut Yuri Gagarin became the first man in space.

It is truly sad that Kennedy did not live to see it, but on July 20, 1969, a stunned world watched Apollo 11 commander Neil Armstrong take that small step for himself—and a giant step for humanity. In so many ways, Armstrong was really leaving a visionary president's footsteps in that dusty trail on the moon.

A Promising New President

While nearly all politicians since Kennedy strive to emulate him—his style, his cadence, and his vision—the nation's forty-fourth president has inspired more comparisons than any of JFK's successors. Only time will tell if Barack Obama can deliver his vision of change and hope with deeds. But there is no question of his promising chance, based upon his truly remarkable campaign for the presidency.

None who compared Obama to Kennedy had more influence than the slain president's own daughter, Caroline. In a rare endorsement so early in a Democratic presidential race, she boosted Obama's fortunes with no-holds-barred support.

In a January 27, 2008, op-ed for the *New York Times* entitled "A President Like My Father," Caroline Kennedy endorsed Obama with words that would have to be the envy of any politician since JFK's time: "Over the years, I've been deeply moved by the people who've told me they wished they could feel inspired and hopeful about America the way people did when my father was president. This sense is even more profound today. That is why I am supporting a presidential candidate in the Democratic primaries, Barack Obama."

Caroline, who was only five years old when her father was assassinated, poignantly noted that "I have never had a president who inspired me the way people tell me that my father inspired them." But in Obama, she wrote, "I believe I have found the man who could be that president."

Obama's appeal to young voters and vision for change in the 2008 campaign certainly recalled Kennedy's embodiment of a new generation. So much about him reminded us of JFK. The elegance and eloquence of his words rang true for voters in ways that seem phony in the person of politicians who try to mimic Kennedy. Even Obama's physicality is similar—a tall, thin frame and a faraway look in his eyes that suggests a thoughtful intellect at work.

There is no question that sophisticated style can make your vision soar, Mr. President. But style is no substitute for a vision that precedes action. Kennedy not only said he would change the world, as Obama promised in his campaign. He actually did it—in just a thousand days of a presidency that fondly became known as Camelot.

Obama's call for change got a head start because he embodies that change. Sworn in as Barack Hussein Obama, his very name represents a dramatic difference compared to all of his predecessors. As the nation's first African-American in the White House, he fulfilled a generation of dreams inspired by the Reverend Martin Luther King Jr.'s vision.

An overwhelming desire for change, combined with Obama's uniqueness as a presidential prospect, allowed him to keep his vision of change somewhat vague in the campaign. Voters were so desperate for something different that Obama simply was not pressed for specifics. And the news media were so enamored of him that they too did not push for details about how he would govern.

There were clues about Obama's worldview in his book *The Audacity of Hope.* In a chapter entitled "The World Beyond Our Borders," Obama wrote about wanting to end what he considered a long period of divisiveness among Americans about how to conduct ourselves around the world. He described how Reagan's policies disturbed him at a time when he was coming of age as a political activist:

> Looming perhaps largest of all was Ronald Reagan, whose clarity about communism seemed matched by his blindness regarding other sources of misery in the world. I personally came of age during the Reagan presidency—I was studying international affairs at Columbia, and later working as a community organizer in Chicago—and like many Democrats in those days I bemoaned the effect of Reagan's policies toward the Third World: his administration's support for the apartheid regime of South Africa, the funding of El Salvador's death squads, the invasion of tiny, hapless Grenada. The more I studied nuclear arms policy, the more I found Star Wars to be ill conceived; the chasm between

Reagan's soaring rhetoric and the tawdry Iran-Contra deal
left me speechless.

Obama's determination and ability to present a different face
to the world soon became a trademark of his presidency. Halfway
through his first year in office, Obama delivered a powerful call for
unity and understanding to Arab leaders and students in Cairo. The
White House aggressively marketed the speech as the beginning of
an entirely new relationship between the West and the Middle East.

Obama foreshadowed his expansive worldview to an estimated
crowd of two hundred thousand in Berlin during the presidential
campaign, putting into soaring words the thoughts about foreign
policy that he expressed in his book. It was an audacious act. Here
is where John Kennedy and Ronald Reagan had made history with
resounding speeches.

Obama's eloquence in expressing his ideas and his personal experience was a clear call for a new and different future, seeking many
specific changes, from a renewed fight against global warming to
offers of real solutions for ravaged third-world nations. And that is
what vision means:

> I know that I don't look like the Americans who've pre-
> viously spoken in this great city. The journey that led me
> here is improbable. My mother was born in the heartland
> of America, but my father grew up herding goats in Kenya.
> . . . At the height of the Cold War, my father decided, like
> so many others in the forgotten corners of the world, that
> his yearning—his dream—required the freedom and op-
> portunity promised by the West. And so he wrote letter after
> letter to universities all across America until somebody,
> somewhere answered his prayer for a better life. That is why
> I'm here. And you are here because you too know that yearn-
> ing. This city, of all cities, knows the dream of freedom. . . .
> This is the moment when we must give hope to those left be-
> hind in a globalized world. . . . People of Berlin—and people
> of the world—the scale of our challenge is great. The road

ahead will be long. But I come before you to say that we are heirs to a struggle for freedom. We are a people of improbable hope. With an eye toward the future, with resolve in our hearts, let us remember this history, and answer our destiny, and remake the world once again.

"Institutions Must Advance"

Always look forward, Mr. President, project into the next century. Where are our major institutions headed? Whether it is our status in the world, the future of journalism, Congress, the courts, or the presidency, Americans will always face a stream of critical choices that will shape the path that our relatively young democracy takes.

Thomas Jefferson once said, "I am certainly not an advocate for frequent and untried changes in laws and constitutions. But I know also that laws and institutions must go hand in hand with the progress of the human mind. As that becomes more developed, more enlightened, as new discoveries are made, new truths disclosed, and manners and opinions change with the change of circumstances, institutions must advance also and keep pace with the times."

The year was 1816, but Jefferson's words have never been more salient than they are today—and they will probably always be so. In short, with each new president we are likely to need yet another revolution and a powerful vision that makes our lives better and keeps the people in charge of their country.

EIGHT

DO THE RIGHT THING:
YOU'LL NEVER BE WRONG

I brought myself down. I impeached myself by resigning.
—RICHARD MILHOUS NIXON

During the 2008 presidential campaign, Bill Clinton told a revealing story about Barack Obama, one that just about perfectly described how presidents should make decisions.

In a glowing tribute to the Democratic nominee during their joint visit to Orlando shortly before Election Day, Clinton described Obama's measured and thoughtful response to a crisis in the financial markets. In mid-September, the collapse of several large firms created a panic among home mortgage lenders and their borrowers. With rising unemployment and other signs of recession looming, the big-company failures dramatized how the economy suddenly seemed to be falling apart.

All eyes were on the two presidential nominees for a response. Republican John McCain made a strange choice after initially saying the "fundamentals" of the economy were strong. Facing criticism that his seemingly dismissive remark indicated that the wealthy McCain did not understand the plight of average Americans, the Arizona senator reversed course overnight.

McCain stunned the political world by announcing that the economic situation was so dire that he would suspend his campaign and immediately fly back to Washington and work with Senate colleagues on legislation to bail out failing mortgage firms. That did not go over too well either, and he soon reversed tracks again, returning to the campaign trail and distancing himself from the bailout plan.

Obama's response was quite different. He privately studied the problem before he spoke.

"He took a little heat for not saying much," Clinton noted in his Orlando speech on October 30, 2008. "I knew what he was doing. He talked to his advisers. He talked to my economic advisers. He called Hillary. He called me. He called Warren Buffett and he called Paul Volcker. He called all those people and you know why, because he knew it was complicated and before he said anything he wanted to understand."

"We Need a President Who Wants to Understand and Who Can Understand"

That is the first requirement for doing the right thing, Mr. President. Put some effort into studying the issue. Amazingly, some presidents, like George W. Bush, were known for shirking the hard work it takes to comprehensively evaluate difficult choices—as Clinton hinted to the crowd of Obama supporters.

"Folks, if we have learned anything, we have learned that we need a president who wants to understand and who can understand," Clinton said to knowing laughter.

Bush was never one to read long briefing papers. He liked short memos when presented with policy options. In White House meetings his anti-intellectual bent sometimes took the form of kidding experts for being nerds or geeks if their presentations became too complicated. Although it was all in fun, Bush's attitude hardly encouraged aides to provide the resources and tools that he should have demanded in order to educate himself.

Clinton's next observation about Obama's approach to the economic mess illuminated the most critical aspect of presidential decision making.

"The second thing, and this meant more to me than anything else . . . I know what else he said to his economic advisers," Clinton said. He said, "Tell me what the right thing to do is. What's the right thing for America, and don't tell me what's popular. You tell me what's right and I'll figure out how to sell it."

It sounds so simple, but it is probably going to be the hardest part of your job, Mr. President. Figure out what is the right thing to do—and then do it.

Clinton closed his remarks with solid advice for any president.

"That's what a president does in a crisis, what is right for America," Clinton said. "And you know, after this election there are going to be a lot of rough times ahead and you know it as well as I do. You have got to have a president who can understand and then has the fortitude to stand up and tell you, You hired me to win for America. I've got to make this decision now. This is the very best I can do. And I'm prepared to be held accountable."

Sadly, there are many examples of presidents doing the wrong thing. Sometimes they knew it was wrong but made bad policy choices out of fear of the political consequences. In other cases, they just made mistakes of judgment.

List of Shame

A survey of historians organized by the University of Louisville's McConnell Center came up with a list of shame, itemizing some of the worst presidential mistakes of all time. Study this list, Mr. President. You might learn as much from this as you learn from the presidents who got it right.

The top ten worst mistakes:

1. James Buchanan won the dubious honor of committing the worst mistake of all time by failing to avert the Civil War, by not doing enough to oppose efforts by Southern states to secede from the Union. He watched silently as South Carolina seceded toward the end of his presidency, followed by six other states. He took the position that the federal government could not legally prevent a secession, although he refused to legally recognize them.

By the time Abraham Lincoln succeeded Buchanan, the Confederacy was already formed.

Some historians speculate that Buchanan might have gone further and legally recognized the Confederacy as a separate nation. However, several opponents of doing that had taken control of his cabinet and forced Buchanan to reject legitimizing the secession movement.

Although a Northerner born in Pennsylvania, Buchanan personally favored slaveowners' rights, and he sympathized with the slave-expansionists. In his third annual message to Congress, Buchanan claimed that the slaves were "treated with kindness and humanity . . . Both the philanthropy and the self-interest of the master have combined to produce this humane result."

2. The second-worst mistake, according to the university survey, was Andrew Johnson's decision just after the Civil War to side with Southern whites and oppose improvements in justice for blacks beyond abolishing slavery. "We continue to pay" for Johnson's errors, wrote Michael Les Benedict, an Ohio State University history professor emeritus.

While serving as Lincoln's vice president, Andrew Johnson, a Tennessee native, talked a good game when he was called upon to thrash the South. But he considerably softened after succeeding Lincoln following the president's assassination. He advocated a conciliatory approach to the citizens of the former Confederacy. "I say, as to the leaders, punishment. I also say leniency, reconciliation and amnesty to the thousands whom they have misled and deceived," Johnson said.

But Johnson was not even as harsh toward the Confederate leaders as he vowed to be. He allowed the Southern states to hold elections in 1865, resulting in prominent ex-Confederates being elected to the U.S. Congress (although Congress did not seat them).

Congress and Johnson frequently tangled, and in an increasingly public way, about how to conduct reconstruction of the South and could not agree on a process for readmitting the secessionist states to the Union. He ultimately faced two impeachment trials in the Senate, but his foes fell short of the necessary votes to oust him.

Historian James Ford Rhodes writes in his book *History of the United States from the Compromise of 1850* that Johnson was simply stubborn, that he could not bear losing any argument, no matter how minor the dispute. His refusals to compromise prevented sensible policy. Without consensus the postwar period under Johnson descended into chaos.

"His quarrel with Congress prevented the readmission into the Union on generous terms," Rhodes wrote. "For the quarrel and its unhappy results Johnson's lack of imagination and his inordinate sensitiveness to political gadflies were largely responsible: it was not a contest in which fundamentals were involved. He sacrificed two important objects to petty considerations. His pride of opinion, his desire to beat, blinded him to the real welfare of the South and of the whole country."

3. Lyndon Johnson earned the number three worst error in the survey of historians by allowing the Vietnam War to escalate. Historian Andrew Busch: "Neither all the way in nor all the way out, Johnson hoped to muddle through without political mobilization at home—[a] strategy aimed to avoid defeat rather than win a decisive victory. . . ."

For a president who wanted so much to be remembered as one of the greatest, it is truly sad that his mistakes with Vietnam overshadow his many achievements. Indeed, if not for Vietnam, Johnson would be a candidate for a top ten list of great presidents. His "Great Society" legislation created some of today's most popular federal programs, including civil rights laws, Medicare (government-funded health care for the elderly), Medicaid (government-funded health care for the poor), aid to education, and the "War on Poverty."

4. Woodrow Wilson's refusal to compromise with the Senate on the Treaty of Versailles after World War I made the list of worst mistakes. The president's recalcitrance and petty quarrels with Senate leaders is generally cited as the main reason that it was not ratified, leaving the United States out of the mix in European affairs.

5. Richard Nixon's involvement in the Watergate cover-up. You can boil Nixon's problems down to an almost instinctual inability to tell the truth. "You don't know how to lie," he once privately told a political associate. "If you can't lie, you'll never go anywhere." Of course, publicly, he struck a different pose. "Let us begin by committing ourselves to the truth, to see it like it is and tell it like it is, to find the truth, to speak the truth and to live the truth," he said in his 1968 acceptance speech for the Republican nomination.

6. James Madison's failure to keep the United States out of the War of 1812 with Britain. "Britain was reforming its trade policy even as Madison made the choice of war," said Peri Arnold, one of the historians surveyed in the University of Louisville study. "Had he waited and pursued further diplomacy the war could have been avoided. The immediate cause of this error was poor information (due to distance) and, perhaps, bad judgment."

    Another of the historians asked to rank mistakes, Richard Pious, said, "As commander-in-chief Madison did not have to abet a congressional decision to go to war against the British. Moreover, he could have acted as John Adams had done in the undeclared naval war against the French, which was to turn off the dogs as soon as possible and seek a negotiated settlement. This was a war of choice, and a war of aggression against Canada designed for territorial gain that was not essential for our Manifest Destiny across the continent."

7. Thomas Jefferson's Embargo Act of 1807, a self-imposed prohibition on trade with Europe during the Napoleonic Wars. "His embargo almost destroyed the American economy, and in attempting to enforce it he was the only president ever to use the U.S. army against the American people," historian Forrest McDonald said. "The embargo's effect was that of a flea trying to stop a dog-fight by threatening suicide."

    Historian Marshall DeRosad agreed that the embargo "severely impacted the U.S. economy in a negative way, without achieving the desired foreign policy objectives. More significantly, the embargo ushered in the protectionism for northeast industries, which resulted in the subsequent tariff controversies between the north and south."

8. John Kennedy allowing the ill-fated Bay of Pigs invasion to overthrow Cuba's communist government that led to the Cuban missile crisis. Historian Shirley Warshaw: "The failure of President Kennedy to thoroughly question the CIA in 1961 on the Bay of Pigs invasion to topple Fidel Castro led to escalating tension with Cuba and their alliance with the USSR, an alliance which led the USSR to place missiles in Cuba. The Cuban Missile Crisis ensued, with the potential for nuclear war."

Other historians on the Bay of Pigs:

James Piffner: "The invasion by Cuban exiles gave Khrushchev the excuse to insert nuclear-armed missiles in Cuba, leading to the Cuban Missile Crisis of 1962. Nuclear war was narrowly avoided."

Matthew Dickinson said the U.S.-backed invasion was "rooted in arrogance and tinged with hopefulness, but JFK learned never to rely solely on his military experts again."

9. Ronald Reagan and the Iran-Contra affair, the effort to sell arms to Iran and use the money to finance an armed anticommunist group in Nicaragua. "How shameful! Selling arms to a terrorist nation, then using the profits to violate the law," Michael Genovese said.

Andrew Dowdle: "While it did not lead to the same institutional diminishment of power that Watergate did, Iran-Contra stopped the recovery of public trust in the presidency that Reagan had successfully achieved."

Matthew Dickinson: "Although Reagan handled the aftermath in textbook fashion—no hint of cover-up—the initial decision to swap arms for hostages betrayed a surprising lack of political sensitivity—there was no pressing need to do this."

10. Bill Clinton's Monica Lewinsky scandal. "Great political skills compromised by constant personal scandal," Robert Levy said. "The mistake is what he could have accomplished for the Democrats, and the nation, without the monumental character flaws. The personal self-destruction of a potentially great presidency."

Ryan Barilleaux: "Had Clinton been a man of integrity, he would have resigned after the affair became public. The country could have been spared the whole affair and subsequent impeachment. What a waste."

Will George W. Bush's decision to invade Iraq make the list someday? "We're going to have to wait a few more years before we can decide where it belongs," said Michael Nelson, a political science professor at Rhodes College in Memphis, Tennessee

Nelson pointed out that the Iraq War could still end up on a list of good presidential decisions. "The fact that we don't know shows you how hard it is sometimes to tell how they're going to look with the passage of time. When a president makes a bold decision, it carries great opportunity but also great risk."

Despite so often getting it wrong, presidents are uniquely qualified to do the right thing *for* the whole country because they and their vice presidents are the only politicians in America who are elected by the whole country. That is a fact that every president should repeat to members of Congress and any other politicians who give them trouble when the right thing to do is not the safest political choice. What's best for the entire nation is sometimes not what's best for a particular state or district.

It takes strong presidents to look out for the national interest when special interests would have them do the wrong thing.

The power of the veto is a president's best weapon for special interests on Capitol Hill. It is telling that the first president to extensively use the veto—Grover Cleveland—often deployed it as a tool for fighting corruption in Washington.

"Rugged Honesty in a Corrupt Age"

Few presidents have presided over such corrupt times as Cleveland did. And few so consistently chose to do the right thing in the face of political pressure.

Though often overlooked, Cleveland is widely regarded by historians as one of our most effective presidents. Following a line of weak chief executives in the late 1800s, he restored the power and prestige of the office just in time for the twentieth century.

"Cleveland embodied rugged honesty in a corrupt age," historian Arthur Schlesinger wrote in a 2004 op-ed article for the *Los Angeles Times*.

Mark Twain coined the term for the excesses of Washington, D.C., in the decades just before Cleveland's presidency. He called it "The Gilded Age," the title of his most historically descriptive novel. Twain and co-author Charles Dudley Warner satirize graft, material-ism, and corruption in the nation's public life, borrowing their title from a line in Shakespeare's *King John:* "To gild refined gold, to paint the lily . . . is wasteful and ridiculous excess."

The novel's main theme eerily evokes modern times. It primarily focuses on how a nationwide lust for getting rich through land spec-ulation corrupts society at all levels. A Tennessee family schemes to sell seventy-five thousand acres of unimproved land to the govern-ment by sending their beautiful daughter to join Washington society, with the help of a senator, and persuade Congress to buy the land.

Although it has been more than a hundred thirty years since the book was published, Twain's fictional account of Washington lob-bying, bribery, and cynicism is remarkably contemporary. Even the novel's focus on land speculation evokes the mortgage crises of 2008, as property values spiraled beyond reason while lenders sold and resold loans until it all came crashing down.

The biting sarcasm, hilarious situations, and eccentric characters in the novel tend to overshadow the authors' public policy aims, but their true intent seems to creep out in one somber passage where they wrote, "no country can be well governed unless its citizens as a body keep religiously before their minds that they are the guardians of the law and that the law officers are only the machinery for its execution, nothing more."

Average Americans had become disconnected from governance in Twain's time. He had become a fierce advocate of civil service reform to clean up the mess in Washington that he had described in *The Gilded Age.*

Twain voted for Grover Cleveland in the presidential election of 1884. Although not a member of Cleveland's party, the Democrats,

Twain was horrified by the stench of corruption surrounding the Republican candidate, James Blaine. In a passionate letter to a friend who was supporting Blaine, he argued that Cleveland was essentially the lesser of evils.

"It is not necessary to vote for Cleveland," Twain wrote. "The only necessary thing to do, as I understand, is that a man should keep himself clean (by withholding his vote from an improper man). ... It is not parties that make or save countries or that build them to greatness—it is clean men, clean ordinary citizens, rank and file, the masses. Clean masses are not made by individuals standing back till the rest become clean."

Cleveland had gained a reputation as a reformer for challenging the Tammany Hall political machine in his home state of New York, where he had served as governor and earlier as mayor of Buffalo. But on a personal level he was attacked for having fathered a child out of wedlock.

Cleveland publicly acknowledged, with his typical forthrightness, fathering the child while a lawyer in Buffalo. Opponents popularized the derisive phrase "Ma, Ma, where's my Pa?" in an effort to soil his clean image. When campaign aides first approached him with the rumors, he said, "Tell the truth."

Cleveland stepped forward and admitted that years earlier he had paid child support to the mother. It turned out that the woman had been involved with several men at the time and had actually named the child after another of her lovers. Friends said that none of the men knew who actually fathered the child, but that Cleveland took responsibility because at the time he was the only bachelor and wanted to protect his married friends from embarrassment.

Doing the right thing about such a painful and personal matter was also good politics. "His honesty made Cleveland the butt of many jokes, but probably helped him win over voters," historian Robert Allen Rutland concluded.

Cleveland was able to keep the country focused on his reputation as a clean politician despite the jokes about his private life.

Reform-minded Republicans like Twain, who were called Mugwumps, backed Cleveland and helped him become the first

Democrat in the White House since the Civil War, ending the GOP's twenty-four-year dominance that had begun with Abraham Lincoln.

Cleveland moved quickly to clean up Washington. First, he stunned and infuriated the city's powerful interests by shunning their cozy system of spoils for political friends. By his time, the ranks of government jobs filled by presidents had swelled to an all-time high, and these posts were generally given as rewards to their supporters without any regard for their qualifications.

"Officeholders are the agents of the people, not their masters," Cleveland said in a quote that was reminiscent of Twain's statement in his novel that citizens must be the "guardians of the law" and officers the "machinery of its execution." The new president immediately announced that, unlike many of his predecessors, he would not summarily fire members of the opposing party if they were doing a good job. He also said that no one would be appointed based solely on their party service.

Democrats were furious and dumbfounded that a president of their own party would do such a thing. They had been out of power for so long and were chomping at the bit to take their turn at the public trough.

Cleveland went further. Not only did he shut down the spoils system for appointments and require proof of merit for government posts, he began reducing the number of jobs in what had become a bloated federal workforce of political time-servers.

When pressed by angry party leaders to back down, Cleveland remained firm and said, "I would rather the man who presents something for my consideration subject me to a zephyr of truth and a gentle breeze of responsibility rather than blow me down with a curtain of hot wind."

"Our Best Unknown President"

Far from backing down, our twenty-second president unleashed a whirlwind of change throughout government and commerce, leading modern-day historian Henry Graff to conclude in his 2002 biography of Cleveland that he was "our best unknown president."

Cleveland forced America's railroad barons to return 81 million western acres previously granted by the federal government and regulated them with the Interstate Commerce Act. The rights of way for railroad land would be returned to the public, Cleveland announced, because the companies were not extending rail lines as promised and were instead reaping profits from land speculation.

Business interests accustomed to pillaging the federal treasury with questionable deals saw their contracts canceled by Cleveland's administration. For instance, as part of his drive to modernize the navy, Cleveland got tough on construction firms that had been building inferior ships, putting several out of business.

Doing the right thing by taking on such powerful interests came at a cost, however. He lost the Electoral College vote in his reelection bid despite winning the popular vote. But he returned to the White House four years later, making him the only president to serve two nonconsecutive terms. Since he was both the twenty-second and twenty-fourth president, he will be featured on two separate dollar coins to be released in 2012.

Many presidents take office vowing to clean up Washington. Ronald Reagan famously said he had come "to drain the swamp." But few actually kept their promise as well as Cleveland did.

Doing the right things should be easy, Mr. President, when it is something the public wants, like standing against Washington excess and corruption. Even if the powerful are arrayed against you, popular reforms can be sold to the voters.

But what if the right thing turns out to be something the public is not ready for? That's when leadership is truly tested. Sometimes presidents must look far into the future and see what must be done even if the country resists.

Franklin Roosevelt faced such a dilemma in the early days of Adolf Hitler's rise in Germany. Isolationism had almost become a religion among Americans since George Washington's time. Our first president left office warning the nation "to steer clear of permanent alliances with any portion of the foreign world." At the time, there was much debate about whether to take sides in wars between Britain and France. Washington's words were intended to advise neutrality in that conflict, but became an oft-quoted creed throughout the years for those who argued against a variety of foreign entanglements.

With rare exception, future presidents kept the growing nation's business within its own shores. Most of the exceptions were within or near our own hemisphere. World War I was the first time the nation threw itself into a major foreign conflict, but we entered the fighting in Europe late, sending troops in only during the final year of battle.

As World War I raged, isolationist sentiment encouraged Woodrow Wilson to run for reelection in 1916 on the promise that we would stay out of the European theater. He pursued a defense buildup but labeled his policy "armed neutrality." Wilson won a narrow victory with the slogan "He Kept Us Out of War."

"Safe for Democracy"

It took a threat to our own borders to reverse the country's antiwar stance. Shortly after Wilson's reelection the nation was outraged by the publication of a secret message from Germany to the Mexican government urging an invasion of the United States. The German message, decoded by the British, promised that, once America was defeated, Germany would force the return of Texas, New Mexico, and Arizona to Mexico.

German submarine warfare in the Atlantic Ocean, which had been going on for many months, was also becoming more active since a hundred twenty-eight Americans were killed in the sinking of the passenger ship *Lusitania* in 1915. But even that incident was not enough to push the United States into the war. At the time, Wilson gave in to isolationist sentiment, saying the country was "too proud to fight."

Shortly after beginning his second term Wilson went before Congress and asked for a declaration of war against Germany to keep the world "safe for democracy." In this dramatic departure from Washington's long-standing policy against getting involved in European wars, the nation's innate isolationism was temporarily overcome.

Clearly conscious of this reversal of American tradition, Wilson forcefully argued the case to Congress for entering what many called the Great War: "Neutrality is no longer feasible or desirable where the peace of the world is involved and the freedom of its peoples, and the menace to that peace and freedom lies in the existence of autocratic governments backed by organized force which is controlled wholly by their will, not by the will of their people. We have seen the last of neutrality in such circumstances. We are at the beginning of an age in which it will be insisted that the same standards of conduct and of responsibility for wrong done shall be observed among nations and their governments that are observed among the individual citizens of civilized states."

World War I had already been waged for three years by the time the United States sent troops. Still tipping his hat to Washington's admonition against "permanent alliances," Wilson was careful to establish that we were not a formal member of the Allies, instead labeling our role as that of an "Associated Power." A year later the war was over.

Below the surface, the Wilson administration had worked very hard to change the nation's antiwar stance while publicly playing to that sentiment. There were propaganda campaigns, manipulation of newsreels, and many excesses in targeting and harassing antiwar groups.

Wilson clearly thought the country needed to get involved but was afraid to say so until after his reelection. It was his own White House, by the way, that released the secret message from Germany to Mexico in an effort to fan the flames for war.

Doing what he thought was the right thing when the public will was against it led Wilson to play a lot of tricks, fooling voters in his reelection campaign and presiding over a rather underhanded series of steps to alter public opinion.

Make Your Case

If you think we must go to war, Mr. President, why not just say so and let the chips fall where they may? If it is the right thing, then you ought to be able to lead the country with forthrightness. Make your case. If it is a strong one, you should prevail.

Franklin Roosevelt looked at Wilson's experience and knew that, once again, war against Germany was inevitable. But he too could not find the political will to get involved until the country was sufficiently engaged to overcome its natural isolationism.

The bombing of Pearl Harbor became the catalyst for America's involvement in World War II. But long before the attack, Roosevelt was actively getting involved.

For a while, the Roosevelt administration viewed the Nazis as a harmless bunch of fanatics who would only annoy Europe. But that changed in 1938, a year before World War II officially began with Hitler's invasion of Poland. German-backed fascists in Brazil led a failed coup attempt. This convinced Roosevelt that Hitler had global aims, that even if the German dictator initially confined his aggression to Europe, he could well become an American problem.

Still, Roosevelt was not ready to publicly say so. He even disavowed remarks made by the American ambassador to France that stirred much speculation about the United States entering the hostilities. "France and the United States are united in war and peace," said Ambassador William Bullitt, a close friend of Roosevelt's.

Although at the time Roosevelt was already engaged in a variety of behind-the-scenes moves toward American participation, he completely rejected such a prospect during a press conference in September of 1938. He called Bullitt's statement "100% wrong" and vowed that the United States would remain neutral and not join a "stop-Hitler bloc" under any circumstances. The very next month Roosevelt opened secret talks with France to set aside American neutrality laws and sell American war planes to the French.

Roosevelt secretly began an arms buildup, much as Wilson had done. In addition to arranging for aircraft to be built and sent to the British and the French, he accelerated a program to build long-range submarines.

When war finally broke out in Europe, to his credit Roosevelt did not fully duplicate Wilson's claims of neutrality before entering World War I. Roosevelt began more openly looking for ways to militarily help Britain and France while backing away from any thoughts of a declaration of war.

Roosevelt was still waiting for American public sentiment to shift away from isolationism, still wary of the political costs to his presidency if he moved too quickly.

Germany's occupation of France in 1940 shocked the country, allowing Roosevelt to become more aggressive. In one of his famous fireside chats, he began arguing the case for the United States to be an "arsenal of democracy," a big step away from his vow two years earlier against joining any stop-Hitler movement under any circumstances.

Germany occupied much of Europe and was bearing down on Britain. By the time of his radio address on December 29, 1940, Roosevelt had already repeatedly defied the Neutrality Acts passed by isolationists on Capitol Hill who were determined to keep us out of the conflict. Two months earlier he had given fifty American destroyers to Britain in exchange for military base rights in the British Caribbean islands and Newfoundland.

Roosevelt knew that much more American help was needed. For more than a year he had secretly been corresponding with Winston Churchill about ways for the United States to help. It was time to finally come out in the open and persuade the nation to do much more.

Still, Roosevelt was keenly aware of sentiment against joining the war. He opened one of his fireside chats by trying to assure Americans that he would resist involvement while implicitly making the case for it: "This is not a fireside chat on war. It is a talk on national security; because the nub of the whole purpose of your President is to keep you now, and your children later, and your grandchildren much later, out of a last-ditch war for the preservation of American independence, and all of the things that American independence means to you and to me and to ours."

While talking about keeping out of war—"our national policy is not directed toward war"—Roosevelt cleverly described the stakes as nothing less than preserving American independence. But then he made a detailed case for how the "Nazi masters of Germany" intended to enslave Europe and use its resources to "dominate the rest of the world."

Throughout this pivotal four-thousand-word fireside chat, Roosevelt repeatedly returned to the point that Germany's goals directly threatened the United States, noting that "some of our people like to believe that wars in Europe and in Asia are of no concern to us." Reading the text, you get the feeling that, like Wilson before him, Roosevelt was talking back to George Washington's stand against foreign alliances.

"It is a matter of most vital concern to us that European and Asiatic war-makers should not gain control of the oceans which lead to this hemisphere," Roosevelt said.

Although it would be another year before Roosevelt asked for a congressional declaration of war, following the attack on Pearl Harbor, he basically called the nation to war in that radio address, prodding the nation to begin making the sacrifices and building the weaponry to win.

"As President of the United States, I call for that national effort," Roosevelt said in the final passage. "I call for it in the name of this nation which we love and honor and which we are privileged and proud to serve. I call upon our people with absolute confidence that our common cause will greatly succeed."

If a president as charismatic and politically skilled as Franklin Roosevelt had to work so hard and so long in private—and sometimes outside the boundaries of the law—to do what he believed to be the right thing, how can less-than-great presidents ever be expected to do so?

"Tell Me the Right Thing to Do and I'll Sell It"

Well, it is your job, Mr. President. As Obama reportedly said to his economic advisers, Tell me the right thing to do and I'll sell it.

Selling the right thing to do is the most important task of any president, particularly when most of the country disagrees. Mr. President, when you face that dilemma—and you will—remind Americans of the many instances when presidents had to lead, prod, and cajole them to do what needed to be done.

Presidents who do the right thing create unforgettable legacies, changing the country and sometimes society itself.

Abraham Lincoln forced a civil war in order to "preserve the union" and avoid what seemed an inexorable path toward becoming a disparate and weak collection of nation-states much like Europe. Civil War historian Shelby Foote points out in the 1990 Ken Burns documentary, *The Civil War*, that before that bloody crucible the country called itself "These" United States. But with Lincoln's visionary leadership and a horrendous loss of lives in battle, we became "The" United States.

Teddy Roosevelt crusaded against business monopolies that had corrupted capitalism, putting the country on a path that one day would allow more Americans to share the nation's wealth. That achievement was nothing short of building the foundation for a middle class that arose decades later, closing the vast gap between rich and poor.

Roosevelt was vice president when William McKinley was assassinated in 1901. Although from a wealthy family, he distrusted rich businessmen of his day, many of whom had been on a binge of corrupt practices despite the efforts of earlier presidents to corral them. He wanted his Republican Party to join the progressive movement that he championed.

Some vice presidents who end up in the Oval Office were passive sorts. Not Teddy. The former "Rough Rider" became one of our most innovative and forward-thinking presidents in history.

The "Trust Buster"

Roosevelt hit the ground running after taking office. His first salvo was a twenty-thousand-word address to Congress that set forth an ambitious agenda that, among other things, called for aggressive regulation of the business world: "The tremendous and highly complex industrial development which went on with ever accelerated rapidity during the latter half of the nineteenth century brings us face to face, at the beginning of the twentieth, with very serious social problems. The old laws, and the old customs which had almost the binding force of law, were once quite sufficient to regulate the accumulation and distribution of wealth. Since the industrial changes which have so enormously increased the productive power of mankind, they are no longer sufficient."

Congress balked, so Roosevelt went another route. He went to court to dissolve forty monopolist corporations, earning his reputation as a "trust buster."

As his popularity grew, Roosevelt was finally able to pressure Congress into action. His biggest success was the passage of legislation empowering the Interstate Commerce Commission to intensely regulate the all-powerful railroad industry. He pushed Congress to pass the Pure Food and Drug Act of 1906, as well as the Meat Inspection Act of 1906. These laws more or less introduced the concept of government protecting consumers. They provided for the labeling of food and drugs, inspection of livestock, and sanitary conditions at meatpacking plants.

Roosevelt deeply believed in building a strong middle class by giving them what he called a "Square Deal" for a better life. "Fundamentally, the welfare of each citizen, and therefore the welfare of the aggregate of citizens which makes the nation, must rest upon individual thrift and energy, resolution and intelligence," Roosevelt said. "Nothing can take the place of this individual capacity; but wise legislation and honest and intelligent administration can give it the fullest scope, the largest opportunity to work to good effect."

Roosevelt almost invented environmentalism. He was the first American president to champion the efficient conservation of national resources. He created the first National Bird Preserve, in Florida, which was the beginning of the Wildlife Refuge system that spread throughout the country. He prodded Congress to establish the United States Forest Service. He set aside more land for national parks and nature preserves than all of his predecessors combined—194 million acres. In all, by 1909, Teddy Roosevelt's administration had created an unprecedented 42 million acres of national forests, fifty-three national wildlife refuges, and eighteen areas of "special interest," including the Grand Canyon.

Although Roosevelt's tireless devotion to his many causes won him great popularity among the masses, the elites in the business and political world grew weary of his reformist zeal. He won a second term, but ended up on the losing side of a nasty rift within his own party. Later, when he decided to try for the White House again, Roosevelt had to run as a third-party candidate and didn't make it.

Still, Teddy Roosevelt is one of the most encouraging examples of a president who politically flourished by never fearing the political consequences of taking on powerful elites.

"I Am Not Going to Let Them Build Up the Hate"

Lyndon Johnson's championing of civil rights was a rare instance of a president doing the right thing while knowing that it was, at least in the short term, a political loser. He correctly predicted that the passage of civil rights legislation would be disastrous in the South for his party. But LBJ was determined to make equality for African-Americans part of his legacy. It made him angry that so many whites in his native South turned against him for it, and he really showed his fury one day while campaigning there during the election of 1964.

Johnson's wife, Lady Bird, had been campaigning for her husband throughout the region. It was a grueling trip lasting 4 days and traveling 1,682 miles from North Carolina to Louisiana with 67 stops for speeches in 7 states. In the election later that year, the Republican nominee, Barry Goldwater, won 5 of those states.

It was not just the physical toll that made the trip difficult for Lady Bird. Her husband's civil rights bill had the region up in arms and many racist whites were eager to show their displeasure. She was met with catcalls and signs proclaiming things like "Fly Away Black Bird."

The First Lady kept her composure. To one protester she said,

"In this country we have many viewpoints. You are entitled to yours. Right now, I'm entitled to mine."

Mrs. Johnson had tried to meet the issue head-on in her speeches. "I know that many of you don't agree with the civil rights bill, or the president's support of it," she said. "But I do know the South respects candor and courage and I believe he has shown both. It would be a bottomless tragedy for our nation to be divided."

But her reception throughout the trip made it obvious that her husband had lost crucial support, even though her grace and good nature under the pressure greatly impressed many. Other signs that frequently appeared in her crowds: "Sold on Goldwater" and "We Want Barry."

By the time Lady Bird reached New Orleans, where she was scheduled to meet her husband, the president had heard about the difficult time she had. In a remarkable speech, Johnson bared his anger at the racist attitudes of some of his fellow Southerners. He complained about how voters were often exploited by white politicians appealing to antiblack prejudice. "All they ever hear at election time is 'nigger, nigger, nigger.'" The official White House transcript changed the word to "negro," but that is not what he actually said.

The rest of Johnson's campaign speech included a powerful and eloquent plea for reconciliation. It stands today, more than four decades later, as an inspirational touchstone for how a truly brave and passionate president can do the right thing, whatever it might be, against the political odds:

> Now, the people that would use us and destroy us first divide us. . . . But if they divide us, they can make some hay. And all these years they have kept their foot on our necks by appealing to our animosities, and dividing us. . . . But I am not going to let them build up the hate and try to buy my people by appealing to their prejudice. . . . I hope if you do what you think is right, that somehow or other it is the same thing that I think is right. But if it is not, I won't question your patriotism, I won't question your Americanism, I won't question your ancestry. I may quietly in the sanctity of

our bedroom whisper to Lady Bird my own personal opinion about your judgment.

Fight Your Fear, Mr. President

If only Johnson had lived to finally see the day that his beloved Democratic Party nominated and the nation elected our first African-American president. By fighting against, instead of fearing, the short-term consequences, Johnson did the right thing.

Fearing the political consequences too often keeps our presidents from doing the right thing for the country. Winning that second term does not always mean you were great, Mr. President.

George W. Bush allowed a culture of spending and corruption that cost his party control of Congress, encouraged corporate excess, and bankrupted the federal treasury.

Bill Clinton was afraid to keep pushing for the expansion of health care to all Americans after the bruising congressional battles in his first term, denying himself the potential for a great legacy.

Richard Nixon's obsession with winning an unprecedented margin of victory for his reelection cost him everything. His lawless campaign tactics and the cover-up he directed brought him down.

Risking your own political fortunes might be required, Mr. President, when it comes time to do the right thing. So what if you lose reelection. You'll probably live longer.

NINE

PAY ATTENTION:
AND YOU WON'T BE SURPRISED

*To those Americans whose support I have yet to earn, I may not have
won your vote tonight, but I hear your voices. I need your help. And I
will be your president, too.*

—BARACK OBAMA

Mr. President, maybe you don't want to listen to us, but you
should listen to the people around you. Just be careful
who you pick.

Surrounding yourself with the right people and listening to good
advice should be your top priority. So many presidents learned that
lesson the hard way. Some paid no attention, while others listened to
the wrong people.

There are many whose opinions you should heed. Widen your
circle beyond your immediate staff. Build strong relations among
foreign heads of state. Develop close ties to influential members of
Congress. Find creative ways to avoid depending solely on pollsters
to understand what the voters are really thinking.

"Just Look at Some of the Things He Liked to Do"

Ronald Reagan's image guru Michael Deaver was once asked how
the president seemed so in touch with what average Americans were
thinking. Although Reagan grew up in the middle class, he had lived
a long life of privilege as a Hollywood celebrity and California gov-

ernor before entering the White House. And yet he had an uncanny knack for the common touch.

Deaver said that Reagan never really lost his middle-class roots despite living among elites for so long. "Just look at some of the things he liked to do," Deaver said. "At the White House, instead of going out to fancy parties, he and Nancy much preferred to eat dinner on TV trays in the living quarters and watch the same prime-time shows that the rest of the country was watching."

Not a bad idea, Mr. President. Keep in touch by watching sitcoms, reality shows, or whatever else is popular on television. Apparently, it helped Reagan win two terms.

Reagan did come across as more interested in average people than in talking to the rich and powerful elites who surrounded him. Occasionally, this trait befuddled others. One of those occasions was in Atlanta when Jimmy Carter was giving Reagan a tour of his newly opened presidential library. Accompanied by an entourage of ambassadors and other dignitaries, Carter stopped at each exhibit to describe them in great detail to Reagan. Reagan politely nodded his head, said very little, and was clearly not as fascinated as Carter probably thought he should be. A former Carter White House aide even murmured to an associate, "Reagan seems really out of it."

But as the group was about to move outside for the speechmaking, Reagan stopped to greet a uniformed security guard employed by the library. The two struck up a lengthy conversation. It turned out that the man had just moved to Atlanta from a town in Illinois near Reagan's birthplace and the president wanted to know all about it. They talked about local sports teams, the weather, you name it. Reagan talked to that lowly security guard for a much longer time during that tour than he did with anyone else, including Carter.

Paying genuine attention to the occasional average American is worth your time, Mr. President. After all, they are more like most voters than the elites who surround you every day.

It is also a good idea to establish a few close advisers outside of government. Bill Clinton was well served by James Carville's choice not to take a job in the White House after running his successful 1992 campaign. But the two frequently talked on the phone throughout Clinton's presidency.

It never hurts to get advice from someone who is not inside the White House bunker, but instead circulating in the outside world monitoring the public mood.

The best presidents often had better instincts about average Americans than the people around them. If you are one of those, Mr. President, listen to your own counsel.

"The People I'm Going to Talk to Don't Know Who Voltaire Is"

Lyndon Johnson had little patience for lofty thinking that was out of touch with common folk. No one in his White House was better connected than he to the sensibilities, language, and thinking of average voters. One of his speechwriters learned this fact the hard way.

The writer showed up in the Oval Office with a speech that Johnson had ordered and the president erupted almost as soon as he looked at it. The text included a quote from the French essayist Voltaire and Johnson was not happy.

"Voltaire!" Johnson shouted. "Voltaire? The people I'm going to talk to don't know who Voltaire is."

The president grabbed a pen and scratched out Voltaire. Then he scribbled in a different citation for the same quote: "As my dear old daddy used to say . . ."

Listener in Chief

Knowing the right words to say matters, but presidents also need to be champion listeners. Often, however, the massive ego it takes for someone to make it to the White House gets in the way of nurturing this skill.

Listening can be a useful tool. You learn more by listening than by talking. Presidents sometimes talk too much, especially in public.

Although as journalists we advocate as much presidential talking as possible, it might not necessarily be good for them.

Calvin Coolidge once said, "The words of a president have an enormous weight and ought not to be used indiscriminately." Our thirtieth president, while perhaps not one of the greatest, was probably the best listener. So much so that he was widely known as "Silent Cal."

Although Coolidge was an effective public speaker, in private and in White House meetings he took care not to tip his hand by saying too much. An unconfirmed story about the quiet Coolidge and the writer Dorothy Parker at a dinner party became a national favorite.

"Mr. Coolidge, I've made a bet against a fellow who said it was impossible to get more than two words out of you." His famous reply: "You lose."

Despite his reputation, Coolidge pleased journalists of his day as one of the most forthcoming presidents ever to serve. During his six years in the White House he held an unprecedented five hundred twenty press conferences and was the first president to allow follow-up questions.

Powerful politicians often seem to think that doing all the talking puts them in control. That is not always the case, especially for presidents.

Teddy Roosevelt was talking about foreign relations when he said, "Walk softly and carry a big stick," but that notion applies more generally. The power of the presidency is a very big stick. Let it speak for itself, Mr. President.

Listening to others not only allows you to learn much more about their needs, motivations, and intentions, it can also make others more loyal by encouraging them to believe you value their opinions. And it prevents them from truly knowing what you think, which preserves your options. The more you know about others and the less they know about you, the better you will be able to control them—or avoid being controlled.

Most important, Mr. President, if you are listening to good advice, you might avoid mistakes.

John Kennedy always regretted letting intelligence advisers talk him into the Bay of Pigs fiasco early in his presidency. Although publicly he took full responsibility for the botched invasion of Cuba, he held a private grudge against those advisers for the rest of his term.

Paying better attention to what you've inherited from your immediate predecessor was a lesson JFK learned the hard way.

Avoiding the Traps

Every new president should be leery of potential traps left over from a previous administration. It is the first thing you should pay attention to, Mr. President.

Dwight Eisenhower initially approved the invasion of Cuba in March of the year that Kennedy was then just a presidential candidate. The Central Intelligence Agency had proposed to equip and train Cuban exiles for an attack against the new communist government led by Fidel Castro. CIA officials were convinced that they could overthrow the Cuban dictator based upon their success in ousting hostile governments in Iran and Guatemala earlier in Eisenhower's presidency.

Preparations were well under way by the time Kennedy took office, and just three months later the invasion attempt took place. The American-trained forces were overwhelmed within a few days, and the new administration suffered a horribly embarrassing loss just as it was getting started.

Some blame Kennedy for refusing to order American air support for the invading forces, but the plan's failure also stemmed from a variety of other factors, including intelligence leaks and the faulty assumption that large numbers of Cubans would rise up to support their "liberators."

Sound familiar? "My belief is we will, in fact, be greeted as liberators," Vice President Dick Cheney said in 2003 as the United States invaded Iraq. It turned out the reception was more like the Bay of Pigs.

The incorrect assumption about a Cuban uprising to help American-backed liberators was later cited by the CIA in its report on what went wrong in the Bay of Pigs. The agency blamed its own internal incompetence for the disaster.

To his credit, Kennedy publicly accepted the blame for the Bay of Pigs defeat. Perhaps too much so. And for decades it became a political problem for Democrats.

Cubans who had fled to south Florida and were angry at Kennedy's handling of the invasion to liberate their former country became a powerful voting bloc for Republicans. And the GOP platform in the next election took full advantage of the situation: "This Administration has forever blackened our nation's honor at the Bay of Pigs, bungling the invasion plan and leaving brave men on Cuban beaches to be shot down. Later the forsaken survivors were ransomed, and Communism was allowed to march deeper into Latin America."

Few presidents ever inherited such a miserable trap as Kennedy's first crisis, but his experience should be a cautionary tale for paying exceptionally close attention to what the last administration left behind.

And yet the very next president after Kennedy—Lyndon Johnson—made the wrong choices about a foreign adventure that he inherited. There was only limited military action in Vietnam when LBJ took office, but the path toward war had begun under Eisenhower and Kennedy.

Johnson had the opportunity to reverse course, but chose to expand what his predecessors had begun. As with Kennedy's experience with the CIA, Johnson always regretted paying too much attention to the military hawks around him.

Getting out of Vietnam became more and more difficult as Johnson upped the ante. After years of the low-profile presence of U.S. military advisers there, in 1965 he sent major American combat units to Vietnam, kicking off a huge U.S. investment in Southeast Asia. As the war dragged on, Johnson agonized over how to end the conflict. In the end, he was forced to abandon seeking reelection.

A Torturous Finale to War

Richard M. Nixon was Johnson's successor and he announced that his plan to end the U.S. involvement in the war was to turn the war over to the South Vietnamese in 1973. The torturous finale came two years later, when North Vietnamese troops defeated the South Vietnamese military and captured Saigon.

Both Nixon and Johnson dithered between advice to escalate and advice to withdraw. Author Otto J. Lehrack wrote about the presidential dilemma of Vietnam in his 2004 book *The First Battle: Operation Starlite and the Beginning of the Blood Debt in Vietnam*. Lehrack makes the point that U.S. withdrawal from Vietnam could have been easily accomplished—without much furor—before August 1965.

But then came the first major marine battle against the Viet Cong at Chu Lai. The Americans vanquished the Viet Cong but suffered 54 casualties. The U.S. toll quickly escalated in later months and, by the end of 1965, American dead in Vietnam totaled 2,385.

From then on, American presidents found it politically, morally, and emotionally difficult to disengage because of what Lehrack calls the "blood debt" that the U.S. leadership had incurred as a result of these casualties and the thousands that followed. How could U.S. officials tell the next of kin and the American public that their loved ones died in a futile war?

"How could the American president defend the expenditure of more than two thousand American lives with nothing to show for it," Lehrack writes. "Like gamblers who have already lost their gambling money, and then the rent money, and then the car payment, and then the grocery money, and then borrowed or stole in the hope of changing their luck, the Johnson and Nixon administrations kept signing markers to America for a debt in gore that they hoped a reversal of fortune would justify."

Three presidents in a row, failing to pay attention and compounding their predecessors' mistakes, led to one of the most colossal and costly failures in our history. Once the tragic path in Vietnam had begun, America spent another ten years and more than fifty-six thousand additional lives in pursuit of the Kennedy-Johnson-Nixon policy in Vietnam.

None of those presidents wanted to be the one who gave up, to tell American families that their sons and daughters died for a terrible, tragic mistake. Yet history shows that other presidents have found ways to end discouraging involvements in foreign conflicts.

After 241 marines and sailors were killed when the U.S. Marine outpost in Beirut was blown up in October 1983, Ronald Reagan said the United States would not change its policy. But by April 1984, Reagan had quietly ordered all American forces out of Lebanon.

There were no public recriminations about cutting and running—only a sense of relief.

Eisenhower promised during his 1952 presidential campaign "to go to Korea" and end an unpopular war that had begun in 1950 when North Korea invaded South Korea. The American people wanted out, so Eisenhower's message resonated with voters and he won the presidency. The war ended in a stalemate with a divided Korea in 1953—and there are still some twenty-seven thousand American troops stationed on the peninsula.

There are too few examples of new presidents, like Eisenhower, taking firm steps to fix something that went wrong before them.

Listen to Your Own Instincts

Don't just go along with what you inherit, Mr. President, if your instincts say otherwise. Even the most confident new occupants of the Oval Office feel a bit daunted at first, preferring to let the Establishment have its way until they get their bearings.

The danger for a new president is that oftentimes the outgoing administration becomes overly aggressive on some matters in a last-ditch effort to add a few more historical footnotes to its legacy. Eisenhower, for instance, wanted to be remembered for his containment of communism, approving the invasion of Cuba during his last months in office. He was most unhappy about losing such a close neighbor to the communists on his watch.

Still, presidents ought to put such projects on hold when they emerge so late in their terms, except in the most dire circumstances.

Sometimes presidents simply cannot finish what they started. George W. Bush left a war in Iraq to Barack Obama, unwilling to draw it down, instead leaving a massive force of American troops on the ground.

Bush's war in Iraq is one of the most tragic examples of a president failing to pay attention to good advice. He ignored Secretary of State Colin Powell's famous warning about Iraq: "You break it, you own it." Despite publicly saying he would listen to his military leaders before making important decisions, in private Bush only wanted to hear what he wanted to hear. Those who disagreed were let go.

A Telling "Distraction"

There were those in government who tried to stop the madness. Consider Admiral William Fallon, who tried to prevent a widening of conflict with Iran. After serving one year as commander of U.S. Central Command, Fallon resigned in the spring of 2008 saying he was quitting because his differences with official U.S. policy had become a "distraction."

The perception in Washington was that Fallon was undermined by the neoconservatives among President George W. Bush's aides, especially Vice President Dick Cheney, because of Fallon's reluctance to go along with the administration's hawkish moves toward Iran.

Cheney, who took five consecutive draft deferments to stay out of the Vietnam War, does not mind keeping the United States in the Iraqi quagmire he helped create—and eagerly beat the drums behind the scenes for saber rattling against Iran.

As head of Centcom, Fallon's command ran from the Mediterranean to South Asia and included Iraq, where he ran afoul of army general David Petraeus, the top U.S. military commander there.

Petraeus was hired to essentially maintain the 130,000 pre-surge U.S. troop level in Iraq for the remainder of the Bush presidency. Fallon was concerned that keeping so many troops in Iraq could leave the United States unprepared for any new crises that might occur elsewhere. Long after Fallon was out of the way, Petraeus did his job, presenting numerous reports to Congress containing upbeat assessments of how things were going. Petraeus played ball and gave the president the answers he wanted.

The Bush White House defused the potential fallout from Fallon's blunt departure with a public relations offensive led by Petraeus. And then they pretended that there was no real disagreement with Fallon.

Defense Secretary Robert Gates delivered the final blow to any hopes that Fallon's pronouncements would sow doubts about the administration's disastrous course. "Admiral Fallon reached this difficult decision on his own," said Gates. "I believe it was the right thing to do, even though I do not believe there are, in fact, significant differences between his views and administration policy." The Pentagon chief, who has held top jobs in government for years, is a survivor who learned long ago to ride the right horse. He praised Fallon, saying he was "enormously talented and very experienced, and he does have a strategic vision that is rare."

While the differences between Fallon and the bellicose White House were well known, they came to a head in an article in the April 2008 issue of *Esquire* magazine written by Thomas Barnett, a former professor at the Army War College. In the article, Fallon appears to be a military man with peaceful intentions. He is quoted as saying, "What America needs is a combination of strength and willingness to engage."

Barnett also wrote that if Fallon left his job anytime soon, it could signal that Bush intended to go to war with Iran. Gates called that assertion "just ridiculous."

Fallon was a rarity in the top military ranks. To tell the truth to the commander in chief often has a price. Just ask Colin Powell, who put aside his personal reservations and sacrificed his credibility when he spoke to the United Nations on February 5, 2003, and delivered a pack of falsehoods to justify the U.S. attack on Iraq. Powell later called it a "blot" on his career.

Yet Fallon's resignation and unusually public split with the administration he served failed to produce a turning point. Although more and more Americans began expressing unhappiness with the hawks in Washington, a White House obsessed with secrecy and skilled at public relations was able to thwart any hopes of changing U.S. policies.

Bush also failed to pay attention to a chorus of world opinion against him. He seemed to adopt the haughty view that power makes right.

American presidents are often quick to think that our immense military power should make the rest of the world do what we say. It's not till they leave office that many have regretted their reliance on military options.

Listen to Your Predecessors

It would be wise, Mr. President, to pay attention to former presidents who learned caution about the often illusory nature of so-called military solutions.

Bill Clinton and Jimmy Carter tangled over such a question in Haiti, producing one of the most melodramatic episodes ever witnessed between a president and one of his predecessors. In the end, lives were saved because Clinton deferred to Carter's judgment.

Haiti's military dictatorship was in Clinton's crosshairs in 1994. It was early in his first term and Clinton wanted to show some toughness by ousting the bloodthirsty regime. A military invasion plan was prepared, but before Clinton took action, Carter convinced the president to let him lead a diplomatic mission to negotiate a solution.

Carter was joined by Colin Powell and former senator Sam Nunn (D-Ga.). When their efforts to persuade the Haitian military bosses to restore democracy failed to succeed before the president's deadline had passed, Clinton order the launch of an invasion.

Planes loaded with American paratroopers were in the air. Warships drew closer. The Navy SEALs were dispatched. But there was a problem. Carter would not leave and instead kept negotiating. Naturally, Clinton was not going to drop bombs on a former president, so he agreed to let his deadline for an agreement slide.

Carter and his team finally persuaded the Haitians to relent. "I told President Clinton that we had an agreement," Carter later told *Time* magazine, "and he turned the planes around."

Suddenly, the troops that had been sent to kill were instead told to go ashore and cooperate with Haitian soldiers for an orderly transfer of power.

Who knows how many would have died that day had a president not paid attention to a predecessor. The incident is also a prime example of how, while the threat of military action certainly helps, sometimes a crisis can be averted by talking to the other side.

The United States should not rely totally on the arrogance of its formidable military power in its foreign relations. There are so many other tools.

Use the Culture

Our culture is also a great resource for presidents to use for influencing other nations. American music, art, and film are far better than our weapons for promoting the cause of democracy. That is why a March 2008 performance of the New York Philharmonic in the Stalinist-style closed society of North Korea was such a remarkable breakthrough.

Music is the universal language. In the case of North Korea, the New York Philharmonic's concert might be viewed years from now as the small step that eventually opened the way for more cultural contacts and understanding between two countries that have been at sword-point since the 1950–53 Korean War.

Overwhelmed by the warm reception in Pyongyang, North Korea, Lorin Maazel, the Philharmonic's music director, told reporters: "I think it's going to do a great deal for Korean-U.S. relations. We may have been instrumental in opening a little door." And yet at the time the Bush White House did all it could to downplay its significance. "At the end of the day," press secretary Dana Perino said, "we consider this concert to be a concert. And it's not a diplomatic coup."

How naïve can you get? It most definitely was a coup after years of hostility. The concert was widely hailed as "symphonic diplomacy."

Although it might have been better if the Philharmonic had played George Gershwin's "Rhapsody in Blue" instead of his "An American in Paris," it was still a transforming event.

In that same week, Bush used a news conference to up the ante for threats against others. He dumped a bucket of cold water on any notion that, after fifty years, the United States might soften its policy toward Cuba. "Sitting down at the table, having your picture with a tyrant such as Raul Castro—Fidel Castro's brother and successor—for example, lends the status of the office and the status of our country to him," Bush said, explaining: "He [Raul Castro] gains a lot from it by saying, 'Look at me, I'm now recognized by the president of the United States.'"

The long-standing U.S. political and economic embargo against Cuba was vividly strange when you recall that we have talked to communist leaders from other countries for many years, especially in Moscow, and such talking usually tended toward reducing hostilities and protecting Americans from bloodshed. We talk to leaders around the world, including those in the Middle East who are not exactly models of democracy. But we talk because they are our friends and allies.

Some past U.S. presidents understood the yearning for peace and acted accordingly. When the Cold War was well under way in the 1950s, President Eisenhower said he would go anywhere, any place, any time in pursuit of peace.

Pax Americana may be what some hoped for in pursuing a bellicose foreign policy. But how might history be different if instead Bush had extended an olive branch.

Our leaders must learn what many Americans well know: The United States cannot call all the shots, or pick and choose which leader-dictator we will talk to, or decide which countries can have unconventional weapons.

Avoid Sycophants

Surround yourself with sycophants, Mr. President, and you will not be protected from yourself. You are human. You are fallible. You must make sure to have people around you who test and challenge your ideas.

Just because you are president does not mean you are right about everything.

Franklin Roosevelt made a game of widening the circle of opinion around him. He liked to hear aides argue back and forth, in some ways setting up competitions among them. The various advocates were not always sure which side he was on, which is how Roosevelt liked it.

FDR's internal free-for-all could be a messy process, but it worked for him. He once joked, "Whenever you have an efficient government, you have a dictatorship." By borrowing from a wide variety of sources, he fashioned his own way, always paying honest attention to the actual results of his decisions. And he was not afraid to reverse course if a decision turned out badly.

In a 1936 speech offering advice to young Democrats, Roosevelt summed up his philosophy of making decisions with a timeless gem of wisdom for all future presidents: "In regard to every problem that arises, there are counselors who say, 'Do nothing'; other counselors who say, 'Do everything.' Common sense dictates an avoidance of both extremes. I say to you: 'Do something'; and when you have done that something, if it works, do it some more; and if it does not work, then do something else."

TEN

LISTEN UP, VOTERS:
IT'S UP TO YOU

Sometimes I feel like a fire hydrant looking at a pack of dogs.
—BILL CLINTON

Ultimately, the American presidency is about the American people. It is about the opportunity we are given every four years to learn from our mistakes, and from the mistakes and successes of our leaders. Measuring those mistakes or successes against those of previous presidents is how we make an informed decision about choosing the next president.

While much of this book has focused on how presidents can learn from the past, we also hope it helps voters learn how to choose, how to avoid being misled, and how to hold our leaders accountable.

Those who would presume to lead the world's greatest democracy should be held to the high standards set by our greatest presidents. And we should be on guard against candidates who present too many similarities to our worst presidents.

We believe that John F. Kennedy was our best president of the latter twentieth century, but we lost him too soon to know how much more he could have done—and too soon, perhaps, for him to be considered one of our greatest. Still, his brief one thousand days in office did more good in the world than presidencies that lasted much longer.

We also believe that George W. Bush was the worst president in modern times, but it wasn't necessarily the voters' fault. There is a good chance that he was not the actual winner in the contested 2000 election. You might say he was elected by the Supreme Court.

The lesson here is that you, the voter, not only bear a somber responsibility for making the right choices, you also must be vigilant in making sure your vote counts.

Then, once we choose our presidents, we ought to give them a chance. For the good of the country, even those who voted for someone else should want any president to make the nation better.

Reality Has a Way of Setting In

No matter how excited we might be about the prospects and promise of a brand-new president, history shows that there will be disappointments.

Reality has a way of setting in. The trick is in balancing our expectations and disappointments, never allowing one to overcome the other.

Unreasonably high expectations inevitably lead to disappointment—for presidents and their public. Americans can never resist indulging the hope that a popular new president will change everything and make our problems go away. We might know in our guts that we're expecting too much, but our hearts want us to believe. We need to give new presidents time to adjust, to adapt and find their way. They are not super-human, after all.

The job might be easier on presidents, and the rest of us for that matter, if we tried to be more realistic about how much a new president can really get done and if we remember that something unexpected will likely shake our confidence.

It would help contain expectations if more Americans understood the limits on a president's power and the difficulties in building the coalitions needed to get an agenda through Congress. A good starting place for understanding that is the U.S. Constitution.

"We the People"

The founders of our nation did not design the Constitution solely as a blueprint for our leaders.

Consider its very first words, the Preamble:

> We the people of the United States, in order to form a more perfect union, establish justice, insure domestic tranquility, provide for the common defense, promote the general welfare, and secure the blessings of liberty to ourselves and our posterity, do ordain and establish this Constitution for the United States of America.

"We the people" was not just rhetoric in the minds of those who wrote our Constitution. On the day in 1787 when the framers had finished their work, a well-wisher outside Philadelphia's Independence Hall reportedly asked Benjamin Franklin, "Well, what have we got, a Republic or a Monarchy?"

Franklin's famous response serves as admonition to every American citizen forevermore.

"A Republic, if you can keep it," he said.

When evaluating contenders for the presidency, carefully consider how well they will "keep it," as Franklin warned. How closely will they honor the individual freedoms and limits on governmental power in the Constitution? It is the primary directive in the presidential oath of office: to "preserve, protect and defend" the Constitution.

In examining the careers of presidential hopefuls, carefully examine clues about how they view constitutional limits on executive power. Beware those who either do not seem to understand those limits or come across as cavalier about them.

Also consider how you think they might deal with Congress. It makes a difference in how much they will get done.

As the saying goes, the president proposes and Congress disposes. The most likable, intelligent, and talented leader in the White House will be ineffective without an ability to prod and inspire lawmakers on Capitol Hill to do the right thing.

We Are Who We Elect

American presidents define our image as a nation for the rest of the world. We are a world power, and as such we the people of America bear a responsibility to ourselves and to the rest of the planet to elect presidents who are worthy of that role.

We are who we elect. And there are times when great presidents change us for the better. There are times when we must change as a people, by picking a leader who takes us forward, renewing our nation in ways that keep us current.

No matter how presentable they might be, there will be times when presidents blunder, tell a politically incorrect joke, mispronounce the name of a foreign leader, or even slip and fall down. As human beings, presidents are going to screw up now and then.

The press and the public ought to keep these incidents in perspective, though we might laugh or poke fun, or even get outraged. Unless there is a disturbing pattern at work, we should not make too much of isolated events and let them overtake a president's overall image.

We will always be tempted to dwell too much on every detail of the First Family's private life. They are, after all, part of the image that presidents project. Journalists and citizens alike need to keep this fascination in check.

The health of a president matters. The few examples in our history of presidents who had become nearly incapacitated by illness teach us that in such cases there will be efforts to protect the president's image by concealing the facts.

It is the job of voters to demand an open and responsive government. Be aware that your leaders are often tempted toward secrecy to protect themselves.

Citizens must constantly be on guard against the techniques that our presidents use to deflect, distract, and obfuscate. Blaming the news media for their woes is a clue that your presidents are trying to shift your focus. Limiting their public appearances to gatherings before fervent supporters is another.

Demand that your presidents submit themselves to scrutiny in venues where the logic, truthfulness, and competence of their administrations can be tested.

Do not let your presidents confine themselves to bully pulpits where they only preach to the choir. Pressure them to submit to routine scrutiny, in press conferences or news media interviews.

Be suspicious about a president who refuses to be questioned by objective journalists. He might have something to hide.

The same goes for the officials of an administration. Those actually charged with the responsibilities for governing should be regularly available for scrutiny—not just their spokespeople.

Reward presidents who are open and accessible, and encourage it throughout their administration. When presidents speak off the cuff without a TelePrompTer, give news interviews, or take questions at a press conference, reporters and voters should give them a break if they make a minor mistake and commit a gaffe of some sort.

Too often we pounce so hard on tiny errors in those moments that we force presidents back on script, hiding behind their teleprompters and reading the words of their speechwriters.

It's not easy being president, but the rigors of our election process, while not always producing the best and the brightest, do ensure that they bring some talents to the job.

Great presidents grow in office, developing the courage, vision, and competence to push the country forward in big ways.

What Is a Great President?

Why do we say John Kennedy was our best president in modern times? Sure, there is a case to be made for others. But we make a fine distinction here between our best and our greatest presidents, such as Abraham Lincoln or Franklin Roosevelt.

Lincoln forged a genuine nation out of a disparate collection of feuding states. Roosevelt lifted our spirits, vanquished evil foes, and made our country a superpower. Like Washington himself, they were great and among our best.

Those are daunting competitors for any president who is ambitious to join the ranks of our greatest. Often the times make great presidents—if they are right for the times and up to the challenges they face. Wartime presidents especially have the opportunity to create a positive and lasting legacy.

Our best presidents were not all among the greatest. They did not preside in earthshaking times that etched their names in history books, but they knew how to bring about change that made us better.

Grover Cleveland is overlooked today, but he came along at a time when the White House had been occupied by a series of weak leaders who had allowed the country and the federal government to drift into a wasteland of corruption and greed. Cleveland's personal honesty and civic reforms reversed the country's course when it needed it most, as it prepared to enter the twentieth century.

Teddy Roosevelt introduced environmental ethics, championing national parks and teaching Americans to preserve our land at a time when the dangers of industrial progress were just beginning to emerge.

Woodrow Wilson's passion for making the United States a world leader led us out of our isolationism and paved the way for greatness. His dream of creating a League of Nations fell short at first, but his vision ultimately became a reality with the United Nations.

Harry Truman stands out as a model of character, a plainspoken man whose simple honesty and feisty ways are often cited by today's politicians. The buck stops here, he liked to say about the job of presidential decision making.

Dwight Eisenhower as president could have rested on the laurels he earned as the nation's supreme military commander in Europe during World War II. He could have done nothing and remained popular. Instead, he introduced advances such as the interstate highway system, connecting remote parts of the country to a web of asphalt and concrete that revolutionized commerce and travel for all Americans.

For someone in office for only a thousand days, Kennedy's firm place in history is truly remarkable. He well understood both the tangible and intangible powers of his office. Few presidents, even some of the great ones, fully appreciate their role in our culture, how a president can change society as well as our politics.

It was not just that Kennedy put the nation on a path toward racial harmony, one that Lyndon Johnson advanced with the passage of civil rights legislation. It was not just that Kennedy and his elegant wife, Jackie, opened the doors of the White House to artists, musicians, and other icons of our culture. It was not just that JFK was telegenic at the dawn of the television age.

Kennedy knew how to embody, nourish, and advance what it means to be an American. The rest of the world looked at him and saw all Americans in a different way. They saw that America was the future, that our democracy and respect for civil rights was a path for all nations to follow willingly—and not just because we had the most weapons.

"Peace for All Time"

At a time when the threat of nuclear war was real, Kennedy initiated the idea of negotiating treaties to curb the proliferation of weapons. Until then, world history had been all about building new generations of weapons and using them. For the first time, leaders of great powers stepped back from the brink and broke the vicious cycle.

Plenty of weapons have been made and used since, but Kennedy created an ethos among nations that, while there have been lapses, continues to this day. That next generation of weaponry, the massively destructive powers of nuclear bombs, remained sheathed for the generation that followed him.

Kennedy put the nuclear genie back in the bottle. Let us hope and pray that it stays there. In announcing a test-ban treaty with the Soviet Union in 1963, Kennedy said it best, that the peace he sought was "not merely peace in our time but peace for all time."

To complement the hard bargaining with our enemies, Kennedy created the Peace Corps, which is still a fixture in our global reach. He understood that the world needed more than our military power to follow our lead. He called upon young people to enlist for a different tour of duty, to bring food, medicine, and education to impoverished nations.

For such a young man and a new president, Kennedy was noticeably cool under pressure. During the Cuban missile crisis, when the Soviet Union's installation of bombs in our neighborhood sparked fears of a nuclear conflict, Kennedy managed the challenge to a peaceful resolution.

After Kennedy's assassination, Lyndon Johnson talked to reporters about what he had observed during JFK's marathon White House meetings to handle the Cuban missile crisis. There were many Washington veterans present, some of whom had been serving in powerful jobs when Kennedy was a teenager. But America had never faced such a direct threat to its security so close to our shores, and many of the old pros were unsure about what to do.

"Kennedy was the coolest man in the room," Johnson said. "And he had his thumb on the nuclear button."

Much has been written to denigrate Kennedy's personal life. The press corps certainly looked the other way during his tenure, following the tradition of the time that politicians' private lives were out of bounds unless they affected service to their country.

So despite any personal failings, Kennedy's legacy as a visionary leader is intact. Kennedy's challenge to send astronauts to the moon ushered in an era of technological advance that prepared the nation for the computer age. Nations perish or flourish based upon how well they progress into a new age. America mastered the industrial age in the early twentieth century and, thanks to Kennedy's appreciation for the future of science, we mastered the technological age.

This is what our best presidents do. They prod us forward. They nourish our best instincts. They do not just lead our government. They lead us, make us better, and, as a result, make us a stronger country.

Make Your Vote Count

There is no telling for sure how many Americans regret voting for George W. Bush. His approval ratings in opinion polls during his last year dipped below Richard Nixon's standing when he was forced to resign from office.

The tragic course of the Bush presidency might well have begun as one of the great accidents in American history: his flawed election. It is difficult to find a more dramatic example of why voting matters. It is a moment in our history that should be long studied and never forgotten, lest it happen again. The episode shined a bright spotlight on the flaws in our balloting system. While the machines and the people responsible for them got much of the blame, it was also troubling to discover how many voters simply did not understand how to make their vote count.

It is not enough for you, the voter, to make a wise choice in picking your president. You also must take great care in learning exactly how your polling place works—before you cast your ballot.

Make it a field trip for the kids. Visit your elections supervisor's office on a quiet day before the voting begins and learn all that you can about how your polling place will count ballots. Even if you are a veteran voter, you might be unaware of changes in the machines to be used.

And most important for those who cast ballots where newfangled electronic machines are used, insist that your local government develop a system for paper receipts so that you have a record of your vote in case there are problems.

Remembering what happened in 2000 ought to be enough for all future voters to remain ever vigilant in maintaining the integrity of our polling places.

"Most Florida Voters Intended to Back Gore"

Bush won the Electoral College in 2000 thanks to winning a contested fight against Democratic nominee Al Gore in Florida when the Supreme Court stepped in to stop a recount ordered by state courts. That froze in place the results that gave Bush a 537-vote margin out of 6 million that were cast.

There were 175,000 Florida ballots that year that could not be counted by machines for various reasons. They had to be hand-counted to determine what the voters intended.

One lesson of the Florida 2000 experience is that it is not enough for voters to show up at the polls. You must be extremely careful to properly cast your ballot no matter how confusing it might be.

Another lesson of the Florida recount is that the actual loser might have taken office. We might not ever know for sure, or will we? Florida officials decided to keep the famous ballots for posterity despite an effort by then-governor Jeb Bush—George W. Bush's brother—to destroy them. They can still be counted.

A consortium of news organizations, including national newspapers and television networks, spent months after the 2000 debacle reviewing contested ballots in an effort to find out who actually won. Once the study was completed, the organizations reached different conclusions.

Some reported that Bush would have won anyway; others were not sure. It all depended on what standard is applied for judging a voter's intention.

One of the most troubling issues was so-called overvotes—where it appeared that more than one candidate had been chosen. The cause of the confusion was mostly due to poorly designed ballots.

Gore would have been declared the winner under statewide rules that Florida later developed for evaluating questionable ballots. That was the conclusion of the *Orlando Sentinel*, one of the participants in the consortium study. But those rules were not in effect in 2000, when the standards varied from county to county, so it cannot be said for sure that Bush would have lost if the Supreme Court had allowed a statewide recount.

The bottom line is that more Florida voters tried to vote for Gore than voted for Bush.

"There really is no question that most Florida voters intended to back Gore," said Sean Holton, a Florida journalist who served as an editor in the news consortium's research. The trouble, Holton said, is that so many of Gore's ballots were so flawed that it is difficult to say whether the counting methods of the time would have really changed the outcome. Thanks to the Supreme Court's intervention, that will always be an open question.

There is a disturbing and yet sadly accurate line in the Supreme Court opinion that stopped the counting of Florida's ballots. "The individual citizen has no federal constitutional right to vote for electors for the President of the United States," the Court's majority wrote in *Bush v. Gore*.

This might surprise voters, but, sadly, it is true. The U.S. Constitution gives state legislatures all the power in choosing members of the Electoral College, who technically elect our presidents. Citizens presume to have the power to pick their president only because every state legislature has chosen to give it to them. But it can be taken away at any time—and this should be changed.

That is essentially what happened in Florida. The Republican-dominated state legislature was siding against Florida's courts in favor of Bush and opposing a recount. The U.S. Supreme Court's ruling was partly based upon the fact that under the Constitution the legislature rules in deciding how electors are chosen.

With apologies to legal experts who rightly revel in the many nuances of this case, *Bush v. Gore* comes down to this sobering note: Basically, the Court was saying that Florida did not have to recount individual votes because the individual citizen "has no federal constitutional right to vote" for presidents anyway.

We Need Direct Election of Presidents

Before this happens again, it can be fixed. The Constitution was once amended to change a similar situation. There was a time when U.S. senators were chosen by state legislatures. That was changed in favor of direct elections by voters.

The Constitution must be amended to create what most voters think they already have but don't: exclusive power to directly elect presidents. Had that power been in place for the 2000 election, state officials would have been forced to accurately count every vote and we would at least know who really won.

Instead, we witnessed the installation of a president under a cloud—one who became the worst in modern times.

What Makes a Lousy President?

Historians take a long time to render final judgments. But an early sounding conducted by researchers at George Mason University found sobering results for Bush. More than a hundred professional historians around the country were asked to rank all presidents and 61 percent said Bush was the worst of them all. Even more—98 percent—rated his presidency a failure.

What makes a lousy president? At least three factors were shared by some of our worst chief executives, according to the university study: the paranoia of Nixon, the poor ethics of Warren Harding, and the faulty judgment of Herbert Hoover.

Bush combined all three. His administration was marked by a paranoid obsession with secrecy, a dismissive attitude toward ethics, and a lack of competence highlighted by an ill-conceived invasion of Iraq that led to a miserably managed occupation.

The list goes on. Not only did Bush foster a debacle of foreign policy with a preemptive war, he pursued the demise of basic civil liberties, encouraged dubious torture techniques for presumed enemies, wiped out habeas corpus, and displayed a harrowing disregard for due process and the Bill of Rights.

Grading Bush according to the outline of this book, we find failing scores across the board. Indeed, his presidency provides a textbook case for voters to learn how a president should not behave. In that way, perhaps he offers this lesson as his legacy.

The Bush White House could not let go of its passion for secrecy, never seeming to fully understand that the president is a public servant who owes the nation transparency. Bush ran one of the most secretive administrations in history.

On staying within the bounds of the Constitution, Bush and his vice president thought they were above the law, defying Congress and the courts whenever challenged. The Bush team learned how to cut corners in the 2000 election, avoiding a final recount of Florida's challenged ballots by going to the U.S. Supreme Court to stop it. In many ways that experience produced an attitude that any obstacle, even the Constitution itself, can be circumvented with the right set of machinations.

Bush gets credit for political courage in challenging conservatives within his own party to enact a major expansion of Medicare, providing a means to affordable prescription drugs for seniors. It was a rare instance of going against his political base. But on most fronts, he caved to their every whim.

Doing the right thing did not come naturally to George W. Bush, to say the least. He was too dogmatic. His simplistic philosophy, expressed over and over again in speeches, presented a world that is starkly black and white, good and evil, either you're with us or against us, dead or alive. He reduced everything to such basic parameters that it left no room for a nuanced path to the right decisions.

Perhaps Bush's greatest failing as a president was his refusal to listen, an inability to pay attention to a wider circle of opinion—even from within his own administration. When his first secretary of state, Colin Powell, tried to counter pro-war advice to the president, the former general was sidelined. Political foes on Capitol Hill—Democrats and Republicans alike—were seldom courted, even as a pretense for consensus building.

By the end of his presidency, Bush was as isolated as any president we had seen in a long time. In 2008, no major Republican running for office, from the presidential nominee on down, asked their party's president to campaign for them.

Preying on Our Fears

When Americans are afraid, as we were in those dark days after the September 11, 2001, attacks on our soil, we need a president who reassures us. But the Bush White House used fear of terrorists to get its way. It was a card this president played often, trying to scare the country into following his lead.

It was the opposite of Franklin Roosevelt's uplifting call to optimism in the Great Depression. Instead of saying we have nothing to fear but fear, Bush was saying fear is all we have.

Presidents must not cater to the worst of our nature. Whether we like it or not, sometimes they are there to protect us from ourselves. Before Lyndon Johnson, too many presidents had tolerated or even encouraged racism. He stood up to it in one of the boldest political moves in our history, enacting civil rights legislation and putting the country on the right path.

The press bears some of the blame for Bush's failed presidency. Too many journalists failed to do their jobs when Bush was popular and making the wrong choices. Fearful of being accused of a lack of patriotism or banned from asking questions, reporters kept silent in the White House briefing room during the weeks and months before the invasion of Iraq.

Sadly, too few Americans were pushing the press corps to be tougher. Quite the opposite was true. Reporters who did ask probing questions about the rationale and tactics of the invasion were inundated with hateful mail and calls.

Voters should beware such moments. Even for a president you like and support, you should expect and demand scrutiny of his actions. If he has made the right choices, he should be able to withstand the microscope and, in so doing, strengthen his case.

Only when Bush's popularity waned did the White House press corps get tough and start asking difficult questions. But it was too late by then. The time for skeptical questions was before the invasion, when demanding answers was unpopular. Waiting until it's easy does the country no good at all.

One of the architects of Bush's misadventures did her best to remain confident during his final days in office. Secretary of State Condi Rice, who was his National Security Adviser at the start of the Iraq War, faced a sobering question on *Fox News Sunday* in December of 2008. Was Bush the worst president ever?

"Ridiculous," Rice responded. "I think generations pretty soon are going to start to thank this president for what he's done. This generation will."

Rice was buying time. She noted how the reunification of Germany in the 1990s was rooted in policies going back to the post–World War II era "when things didn't look quite so rosy." She insisted that "one cannot yet judge the effects of decisions that this president has taken on what the Middle East will become."

"I mean, for goodness' sakes, good historians are still writing books about George Washington," Rice said.

Rice is entitled to her optimistic expectations, but at the very least it seems quite unlikely that Bush will ever be lionized as the George Washington of his times.

A Unique and Thoughtful Man

Americans chose change in 2008, picking a president who represents a profound shift from his predecessor in his style, ideals, outlook, and agenda.

So often in our history voters have looked for a new president who is as different as possible from one who has disappointed us.

In Barack Obama we find a unique and thoughtful man who displays the promise to be one of our best. It will take time to know if he can fulfill the promise and match his stirring words with deeds.

As with Kennedy, the world looks at Obama and sees a new America, one that looks more like the rest of the world.

Americans could look at this new president and also see themselves in a different way. It is not just that he is our first African-American in the White House. Or that he is a Christian who happens to be the son of a Muslim-born father he barely knew. Or that he grew up in an unusual mix of places, from Kansas to Indonesia.

Propelled to office by a surge of optimistic new voters and young people, Obama widened the universe of citizens who want to get involved in civic affairs.

No matter what the outcome, the choices you make for the presidency define what kind of nation we are and will be. As a people, who are we? The answer is embodied in the person who occupies the Oval Office.

Our presidents reflect, symbolize, and define who we are—unless by some quirk of history, political machination, or lapse in collective judgment the wrong person goes to the White House.

Usually, it is up to you, the voter. In most cases, if the president goes in the wrong direction, the public bears the responsibility.

Sure, you can say you were deceived—or simply deny that you voted for the bum. It is always interesting how few people admit voting for a president who goes down in the polls. Makes you wonder how they got elected in the first place. Obviously, some people are lying.

Obama has the chance to bring about a new spirit for the country, as Kennedy did. His campaign attracted supporters who had never been active in politics. They learned that being an American is about taking part, that the genius of our nation and the gift of our best presidents is the preservation of a simple ideal: We run our own country.

We do it by choosing the right presidents. To the voters today and for all time, we say: Choose well.

To all those duly elected to sit in the Oval Office, we say: Good luck, Mr. (or Madam) President.

INDEX

About the Authors

Helen Thomas is the dean of the White House press corps. She is the recipient of more than twenty honorary degrees and in 1998 was the first recipient of a prize established in her name by the White House Correspondents Association: the Helen Thomas Lifetime Achievement Award. She is the author of *Dateline: White House, Front Row at the White House, Thanks for the Memories, Mr. President,* and *Watchdogs of Democracy?* She lives in Washington, D.C., where she writes a syndicated column for Hearst.

Craig Crawford is a columnist for *Congressional Quarterly*'s CQ Politics. His writings appear regularly in newspapers and websites, and he is often featured as a news commentator on television and radio. Crawford is the former editor in chief of *The Hotline* and was previously a reporter for the *Orlando Sentinel*. The author of *Attack the Messenger* and *The Politics of Life,* he lives in Washington, D.C., and blogs daily at craigcrawford.com.